Colophon Cafe
Best Cookbook Collection
Three Books in One

facsimile edition
2012
Chuckanut Editions

Copyright @ 2012 by Colophon Cafe
Printed in Bellingham, WA, United States of America

ISBN: 978-0-9860097-4-7

This is a collected facsimile edition of The Colophon Cafe Best Recipes, The Colophon Cafe Best Soups, and The Colophon Cafe Best Vegetarian Recipes. Contents of the original books have been retained in this volume. Each book within this collection has a table of contents and alphabetical index, as well as its own page numbering. Please reference the individual table of contents for each in this collection to locate the corresponding recipe.

Mama Colophon

Best Recipes
of
The Colophon Cafe
Fairhaven, Washington

A Stirring Plot for Cooking Pots,
starring
Quality, Service, Consistency, and Cleanliness!

1208 11th Street (Fairhaven)
Bellingham, Washington 98225
360-647-0092

For more recipes and information, log on to ColophonCafe.com

First published by Mama Colophon, Inc. 1995.
Revised 1997, 2003, 2007, 2011.
This facsimile edition published by Chuckanut Editions, 2012.

These recipes may be reproduced for personal use only.

The who, what, when, where and why of Fairhaven

In 1858, because of the gold strikes in British Columbia, Fort Bellingham, located on what was then Whatcom Bay, found itself the center of about 15,000 people, and the Bay was clogged with ships.

During that manic time, Whatcom Bay was the most convenient port to get goods from the U.S. to Canada's Fort Langley and the Fraser River.

In 1883, a man named Dan Harris, having made his own gold strike by selling rice, vegetables, hardware and hard liquor out of a sloop in Whatcom Bay, bought a claim south of the towns of Whatcom and Bellingham.

Hoping to attract eastern investors, Harris named his claim Fairhaven, built a hotel and began to offer lots for gold. By 1885 he had done well enough to move to Los Angeles!

The real-estate boom of 1888 and 1889 brought Nelson Bennet, a wealthy developer to the area. He brought railroads into town, connecting Fairhaven with Whatcom to the north and with the main line between Vancouver, B.C. and Vancouver, Wash.

Another Californian, Jim Wardner, organized the Fairhaven Water Works Co., the Fairhaven Electric Light Co., the Samish Lake Logging & Milling Co., the Cascade Club and two banks. His 23-room "mansion," Wardner's Castle, is on the historical register.

The Depression of 1893 ended the Fairhaven boom. But coal mines, timber and shipping kept the towns of Whatcom and Fairhaven (which included the old town of Bellingham) going, and in 1904 they merged into a single city, Bellingham.

Taken from Paul Dorpat's "Now and Then," and from the Whatcom County Centennial Committee.

What does it all mean?

COLOPHON: (kol'e fon')

1. A publishers distinctive emblem.

2. An inscription at the end of a book, usually with facts relative to its publication.

3. Greek koloph'on: summit, finishing touch, the last word.

4. The Colophon Cafe is the last word in good eating.

5. Pronounced "Call-a-fawn" Cafe

Mama Colophon

Contents

Savory Soups
The Original African Peanut 9
Split Pea Soup. 11
Colophon Croutons 11
Mexican Corn & Bean Sopa 13
Tomato Parmesan Soup 14
Cream of Broccoli Soup 15
Broccoli Cheddar Chowder. 16
Manhattan Clam Chowder. 17
Gazpacho 19
Curried Corn & Cheddar Chowder 20
Thai Ginger Chicken Soup 21
Polla Tortilla Sopa 22
Salmon Dill Bisque 23
Dutch Tomato Gouda 25
Roasted Red Pepper Soup 26
Spicy Moroccan Bean 27
Sweet Potato Bisque 29

Popular Favorites
Ray's Turkey Chili 33
Curried Carrot & Rice 34
Multi Veggie Chili 35
Turkey Vapata 36
Greek Meat Sauce 37
Broccoli Cheddar Pot Pie 39
Pot Pie Parmesan Biscuit Topping 40
Colophon Pie Crust 41
Pesto Quiche 42
TexMex Haystack 43

Dressing & Salads
Colophon Caesar Dressing 45
Honey Sesame Dressing 46
Fat-Free Italian Artichoke Dressing 47
Jack's Cornet Bay Salad....................... 49
Spinach Salad 50
Hummus 51

Desserts, etc.
Colophon Chocolate Chunk Cake................ 54
Colophon Chocolate Frosting 55
Colophon Peanut Butter Pie 56
Dave's Breakfast Cookies 59
Colophon Cookies .... .60
Bapple Cookies 61
Low Fat Muffins .... .63
Peanut Butter Fantasies 64
The Yogi's Banana Bread .... .65
Old Marge's Cheesecake 67
Apple Crisp................................. .68
Almond-Vanilla Apples 69

Alphabetical Index on page 70.

Mama Colophon

"When you know a thing, to hold that you know it; and when you do not know a thing, to allow that you do not know it — this is knowledge."
　　　　　　　　. . . Confucius

Savory Soups

"Ancient drums echoed eerily through the lush green jungle as a scantily-clad Tarzan carefully stirred the thick soup in his tree-house kitchen, hoping fervently that Jane would swoon over his culinary efforts and melt into his arms in an uncontrollable passion."

From: "Tarzan and the Magic Ginger Root," by Mama Colophon

Mama Colophon

The *Original* African Peanut Soup

This often-copied-never-duplicated recipe was created in the fall of 1985
Ginger root, chilies and garlic give it a distinctive, spicy taste
which some people call addictive!
It has been featured in Barbara Williams' "Coasting & Cooking Cookbook",
along with recipes from the finest restaurants on the Washington Coast.

Blend in food processor:	1 oz. fresh ginger root, scrubbed and chunked 2 cloves garlic 1 tsp. crushed chili peppers
Add to processor and chop, leaving chunky, then add to soup pot.	3-1/4 cups canned or fresh diced tomatoes 1-3/4 cups dry roasted unsalted peanuts 1 medium onion, chopped
Add and cook to 165°:	1-1/2 cups chicken stock 3 cups water
Make a Roux paste. Add to thicken:	1/4 cup flour mixed into 1/4 cup melted butter
Finally, add:	2-4 cups diced tomatoes, canned or fresh 1/2 lb. cooked and cubed turkey or chicken

Whisk warm Roux into soup and simmer to thicken.
Heat to 160°. Add final tomatoes to thin and
to add chunkiness to soup. Reduce heat to 145° to serve.
For vegetarian version, leave out the turkey or chicken,
and use vegetable stock instead of chicken stock.
Garnish with peanuts. Serves 6-8.

As the fog crept across the grey winter
harbor, Captain Vancouver peered out
at the heavily forested coastline, exclaiming,
"Thick as pea soup, this blasted weather!"
Then went below for a pint.

*From "the History of Fairhaven"
by Mama Colophon*

Split Pea Soup

Our simple, healthy version is vegetarian and low-fat . . . and thick as fog! We garnish it with our own homemade croutons.

Lightly sauté in a little butter:
1 cup finely diced yellow onion

Bring to boil. Cook covered on simmer for 1 to 1 1/2 hours, or until carrots are done:
5 cups water
1 lb. green split peas, rinsed
1 medium diced carrot
Salt & pepper to taste

Thin with hot water if needed, but it should be as thick as fog! Garnish with Colophon Croutons.
Serves 4-6

Colophon Croutons

The Colophon's own toasted garlic croutons are great on split pea soup as a garnish, or tossed in a Caesar salad!

Cut enough day old bread to cover a cookie sheet.
Mix together 1/2 cup melted butter with
1 tsp. each of garlic, thyme, parsley and tarragon
Drizzle mixture over bread, stirring as you go.
Put in 400° oven for 8 minutes.
Stir well.
Put back in for 3 to 4 minutes
until they are golden toasty brown.
Leave out to cool.
Store in sealed containers.

"Zapata leapt swiftly from the horse,
stormed into the hacienda,
and after having been gone
six long weeks, strode, not to kiss
his waiting wife, but to the kitchen
for a hearty bowl of soup."

From "Passions of Zapata"
by Mama Colophon

Mexican Corn & Bean Sopa

One of the most popular soups ever to come from the Colophon, the Mexican corn & Bean Sopa has been featured in many publications since we created it. It's vegetarian, low in fat and delicious.

Sauté in a little olive oil:	1 medium finely diced onion 3 cloves minced garlic
Add to soup pot and heat to a slow boil:	1 (15 oz.) can diced tomatoes or equal amount of chopped fresh tomatoes and tomato juice. 2 (15 oz.) cans red kidney beans, drained 1 (24 oz.) can vegetable juice
In a small bowl mix, then add hot water to a paste-like consistency, Add to pot and heat:	3 tsp. chili powder 1 tsp. sugar 1 tsp. cumin 1/2 tsp. black pepper
Add to pot, and heat to 160° Simmer for 1 to 2 hours.	1 (1 lb.) bag frozen corn kernels

*Thin with water or vegetable juice. Garnish with blue and yellow Tortilla Chips
Serves 6-8*

Tomato Parmesan Soup

Friday is always tomato soup day at the Colophon. This Italian flavor soup is easy to make and excellent any day of the week!

In a soup pot, sauté in 1 tbsp. butter or olive oil until tender:
- 1/2 onion, chopped
- 1/4 cup chopped parsley
- 2 cloves minced garlic

Add and heat to 160°:
- 2 (15 oz.) cans tomato soup
- 1 can water
- 1 (15 oz.) canned diced tomatoes, or equal amount of fresh diced tomatoes
- 1/2 tsp. black pepper
- 1 tsp. thyme

Garnish with shredded Parmesan cheese or a sprig of parsley
Serves 4-6.

Variation: If you prefer cheddar cheese, add 1/4 cup of sherry and 1 cup chopped cheddar cheese to the soup mixture, and warm to 160°. Garnish with cheddar wedge instead of grated parmesan.

Cream of Broccoli Soup

A rich and creamy winter's day soup created by the Colophon to make everyone a broccoli fan!

Sauté in soup pot:	1 tbsp. butter 1 medium onion, minced 3 cloves garlic, minced
Add, cover with water, and cook:	3/4 lb. thawed frozen broccoli, chopped
Reduce heat and add:	2 stalks celery, chopped 1/2 tsp. salt 1/2 tsp. pepper Squeeze of lemon Dash of Tabasco
In separate bowl, combine and whip until smooth, then add to soup pot and heat to 160 degrees:	1/4 lb softened cream cheese 1 cup warmed milk
At 160 degrees, add:	Roux: 3 tbsp. flour mixed into 3 tbsp. melted butter

Reduce heat to 145° and thin with milk.

Garnish with cheddar cheese wedge or broccoli crowns.
Serves 8-10

Broccoli Cheddar Chowder

*"It is well known that the cow is a sacred being,"
Ghandi said, "but this cheddar soup does inspire one
to respect it even more."*

Sauté onions & garlic in butter. Put in soup pot:
- 1-1/2 medium onion, chopped
- 1 garlic clove, minced

In soup pot, cook potatoes, broccoli and red peppers, covered in water until tender:
- 3/4 lb. chopped broccoli
- 3/4 lb. chopped potatoes
- 1-1/2 red pepper, chopped
- 3 tbsp. butter

When vegetables are cooked through, add cumin, salt, pepper, dry mustard and flour:
- 1-1/2 tsp. cumin
- 1-1/2 tsp. salt
- 1/4 tsp. black pepper
- 3/4 tsp. dry mustard
- 3 tbsp. all purpose flour

Add cream and cheese until cheese is melted:
- 1 cup heavy cream
- 2 cups grated cheddar cheese

Serve garnished with shredded cheddar.
Serves 4-6.

Manhattan Clam Chowder

For years the Colophon served only a white clam chowder, until we tasted this wonderful red version created by our soup chef. It's spicy, delicious and easy to make.

In soup pot, cook until potatoes are done, in just enough water to cover:

1 diced med. white onion
3 small cubed potatoes
1 peeled, diced carrot
Juice from 2 (6-1/2 oz.) cans chopped clams
1 (8 oz.) bottle clam juice
2 tbsp. parsley
1 diced red pepper
2 tbsp. instant mashed potatoes
1 tsp. thyme
Salt & pepper to taste

Happy as a clam!

Add, heat to slow boil, then turn down to simmer for 10 minutes or so before serving.

1 (14-1/2 oz.) can diced tomatoes with juice
2 cups vegetable juice
2 cans of chopped clams (that were left from the juice you put in)

*Garnish with goldfish crackers.
Serves 4-6*

Dancing clams are fine for the big city, but have you seem our hoofing holsteins?

"Gazpacho!" He declared as his partner sneezed. His friend remembered after that to hold his breath while opening the black pepper.

Gazpacho

A spicy, cold tomato soup, full of healthy veggies. Excellent for a summer meal.

Mix together the day before serving in a large bowl and chill overnight:

3 (15 oz.) cans diced tomatoes, or fresh tomatoes that have been peeled and chopped
46 oz. vegetable juice cocktail
1/4 cup white onion, chopped
3 cucumbers, peeled, seeded and diced
1/2 bunch celery, diced
1/4 bunch cilantro, minced
1 bunch green onions, chopped
2 tbsp. olive oil
2 tbsp. garlic, minced
A good dash of Tabasco
1 tsp. salt
1 tsp. pepper

Thin with chilled vegetable juice if too thick. Chill pot and bowls in freezer before serving. For added flavor, serve with small shrimp and a dollop of sour cream on top. Garnish with tortilla chips.

Serves 6-8

Curried Corn & Cheddar Chowder

The second place winner at the 1986 Chowder Cook Off in Bellingham

Whip together in soup pot:	1 qt. hot water 6 oz. softened cream cheese
Add & heat to a slow boil:	1 (16 oz.) can creamed corn 4 tsp. curry powder 1 tsp. black pepper 1/2 cup chopped onion
Add & heat to a slow boil:	1-1/2 lbs. frozen corn kernels 2 stalks celery, chopped
Add, reduce heat to a simmer:	Roux—3 tbsp. flour mixed into 3 tbsp. melted butter
Stir gently into soup:	1 cup cubed & floured cheddar cheese, tossed and shaken in a bag with 2 tbsp. flour

Garnish with cheddar cheese, grated or cut into shapes.
Serves 6-8

Thai Ginger Chicken Soup

This extraordinary, exotic soup won the 1995 Allied Arts Soup Festival in Bellingham.

Cook until rice is done:
- 2-1/2 cups chicken broth
- 1 cup rice

Add to soup pot, cook until temperature reaches 160 degrees:
- 1 tbsp. "Taste of Thai" Green Curry Base*
- 1 tbsp. garlic powder
- 2 tsp. thyme
- 2 tsp. basil
- 1 tbsp. fresh ground ginger root
- 1 lb. cooked chicken, chopped

Turn heat down slightly and add:
- 1 (14 oz.) can coconut milk
- Dash of lime juice
- Dash of lemon juice

Serve at 150 degrees. Thin with water if desired. Rice will make mixture very thick.

*Curry base contains: chilies, onion, garlic galanga, lemon kaffir, and lime peel. We sell it at the Colophon if you can't find it.

*Garnish with fresh parsley.
Serves 4-6.*

Pollo Tortilla Soupa

The idea for this unique soup was borrowed from a street vendor in La Paz, Mexico.

Sauté onion and garlic in hot oil until onion is tender. Add chicken cook about 5 minutes:	2 tbsp. oil 1 medium onion (diced) 5 cloves garlic (minced) 1/2 lb. chicken (cooked, cubed)
Blend until liquid in food processor, add to pot:	2 (1 lb.) cans tomatoes
Add broth and spices, heat to 160°:	6 cups chicken broth 2 tsp. oregano 1 tsp. cumin 1 tsp. marjoram 1 tsp. thyme 1 tsp. black pepper 1 tsp. salt
For serving:	Mozzarella cheese (shredded) Sour cream Avocado & tortilla chips

To serve, fill soup bowl 1/2 full with broken (not crushed) tortilla chips, cover chips with shredded mozzarella cheese, fill with hot soup.

Garnish with sour cream and/or avocado and whole tortilla chips.
Serves 6-8

Salmon Dill Bisque

By popular demand, a rich and creamy Northwest favorite!

Combine and puree in food processor:
1 carrot, medium
1 red pepper, small
1 green pepper, small
1/2 onion, small
1 celery stalk, diced

Add spices, cover with water and cook until done:
1 tsp. garlic, granulated
1 tsp. dill weed
3/4 tsp. pepper
2 tbsp. lemon juice

Whisk in Roux to thicken:
Roux: mix 3 tbsp. melted butter with 3 tbsp. flour

Turn down slightly and add:
8 oz. smoked salmon, deboned and chopped in food processor

Thin as desired with: 1 pint Half & Half

May be garnished with a dash of dill weed or a fresh sprig of dill. Serves 6-8

A Swishy Wishy?

A cow is a completely automatic milk-manufacturing machine. It is encased in untanned leather and mounted on four vertical, movable supports, one on each corner.

The front end contains the cutting and grinding mechanism, as well as the headlights, air inlet and exhaust, a bumper and a foghorn.

At the rear is the dispensing apparatus and an automatic fly swatter.

The central portion houses a hydrochemical conversion plant. This consists of four fermentation and storage tanks connected in series by an intricate network of flexible plumbing.

This section also contains the heating plant complete with automatic temperature controls, pumping station and main ventilating system.

The waste-disposal apparatus is located at the rear of this central section.

In brief, the externally visual features are:
two lookers, two hookers, four stander-uppers,
four hanger-downers and a swishy wishy.

Dutch Tomato Gouda

This cheesy tomato soup is really a "gouda" Dutch treat!

Sauté onions in a pan:	1 cup onions, diced
Add to soup pot and combine with tomatoes, vegetable juice, water, vegetable base and spices:	11 oz. diced tomatoes, undrained 15 oz. vegetable juice 1 2/3 cup water 2 tsp. vegetable base 1/3 tsp. thyme 2/3 tsp. oregano 1/3 tsp. salt 1/3 tsp. black pepper
Purée one cup of soup and return to pot. Add sugar, and let dissolve:	5 tbsp. sugar
Then add grated Gouda and Half & Half. Heat to 160°.	1/3 lb. Gouda cheese, grated 2/3 cup Half & Half

Garnish with grated Gouda or parsley.
Serves 4-6.

Roasted Red Pepper Cheddar Soup

Another great cheesy soup, but without the tomatoes!

Sauté onions in olive oil. Transfer to soup pot.
- 1 cup chopped onion
- 2 tbsp. olive oil

In soup pot, cook onions and potatoes until potatoes are tender:
- 1/2 lb. baking potato, chopped

Purée cooked potato mixture, along with roasted peppers, then return to soup pot:
- 2 large red peppers, roasted & chopped

Add heated milk, Worcestershire, Tabasco and grated Cheddar. Stir until cheese is melted.
- 2 cups milk, steamed or heated
- 1 tsp. Worcestershire sauce
- Tabasco to taste
- 14 oz. grated Cheddar cheese

Garnish with cilantro sprigs.
Serves 4-6.

Spicy Moroccan Bean

This is one of those exotic soups that everyone wants to try. It's a bit spicy, so be cautious with the pepper, although the milk helps tone it down a bit.

In soup pot, cook onions and vegetable base until onions are translucent.

1-1/2 cups chopped onion
1-1/4 tsp. vegetable base

Add potatoes and beans, cover with water, and cook thoroughly.

3 oz. red kidney beans, drained
1-1/2 cups chopped potatoes

Once potatoes are tender, add spices, soy sauce, milk and potato flakes.

1/8 tsp. black pepper
1/8 tsp. white pepper
1/8 tsp. cayenne pepper
2 tsp. curry powder
1/3 cup soy sauce
2/3 cup steamed milk
1 tbsp. potato flakes

To add thickness, purée about 1/2 of the soup mixture.
Heat to 160°.
Garnish with sour cream. Serves 4-6.

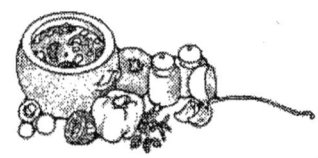

The diner is an American institution. It was started in 1872 by an enterprising peddler with a cart. These lunch carts became walk-in wagons where people could sit down, and were popular all over the Northeast ... so popular and numerous that laws were passed banning them. By 1912, the wagons were turned into permanent structures and the 24-hour diner was born.

Diners were so popular they gradually moved west, and eventually even to Fairhaven. Now we have cafes and drive-ins and espresso stands, but no diners.

There was a certain lingo that servers shouted when placing orders, that evolved out of the diner era.
- Frog sticks! (french fries)
- Nervous pudding! (jello)
- Splash of red noise! (tomato soup)
- Mud! (chocolate ice cream)
- Radio sandwich! (tuna)
- Houseboat! (banana split)
- City juice! (glass of water)
- Baby! (glass of milk)
- Hold the hail! (no ice)
- Sinkers and suds! (donuts and coffee)
- Squeeze one! (orange juice)
- Bossy in a bowl (beef stew)
- Wrecked hen fruit! (scrambled egg)
- Pair of drawers! (coffee)
- On wheels! (to go)
- Bum the British! (toasted English muffin)

And then there is that well loved remark made by an irate waiter ... You Shoulda Had It Toasted!

Sweet Potato Bisque

This bisque is nutty, but good. It would be great for the holidays

---

Sauté butter, onion, leeks, garlic, bay leaf and carrots until veggies are tender:

- 1 cup chopped onion
- 3/4 cup chopped leek
- 1 med. clove garlic, minced
- 1 cup chopped carrots
- 1-3/4 tbsp. butter
- 1 bay leaf

Add sweet potatoes and baking potatoes, vegetable base and water. Cook thoroughly. Discard bay leaf. Purée mixture carefully in a food processor and return to pot. Add white wine and heat to 160°.

- 1-1/2 lbs. sweet potatoes, diced
- 1/2 lb. baking potato, diced
- 1 tsp. vegetable base
- 3/4 cup dry white wine
- 1 cup water

Spread pecans evenly on baking sheet. In a bowl, mix melted butter, brown sugar and paprika. Drizzle over pecans, mix and bake for about 10 minutes at 350°.

- 1 cup pecans
- 1-1/2 tbsp. butter, melted
- 1 tsp. brown sugar
- Pinch of paprika

Garnish soup with the pecans.

Jack Spratt would eat no fat.
His wife would eat no lean.
And so between the two, you see,
... she finally sued for divorce
and with her alimony was able to
buy and eat all the fat she wanted
without having to listen to Jack's
complaints.

Mama Colophon

Popular Favorites

"Most definitely a thumbs up kind of chili," he announced confidently. "And don't even think about putting any cow in it."

From "Get Those Reviewers Out of My Kitchen!" by Mama Colophon

Mama Colophon

Ray's Turkey Chili

*An amazing chili
made without beef or beans!*

Heat oil in a large soup pot and add these, stirring until cooked:
- 3 tbsp. vegetable or olive oil
- 1 chopped red onion
- 1 chopped yellow onion
- 2 chopped leeks
- 6 chopped garlic cloves

Mix these together, adding just enough of the beer to form a thin paste. Stir paste into cooked vegetables:
- 2 tbsp. flour
- 4-6 tbsp. chili powder
- 1 tbsp. oregano
- 1 tbsp. salt
- 2 tbsp. cumin powder
- 1 to 2 tsp. cayenne pepper
- Bottle of cold beer

Add and stir well:

- 3 lbs. cooked chopped turkey breast
- 2 (14 1/2 oz.) cans stewed tomatoes (with juice)
- 1 (14 oz.) can tomato sauce
- 4-5 tbsp. of the beer (drink the rest)
- 1 tbsp. peanut butter

*Stir often and simmer on low heat 2-5 hours. Add beer or water to thin, but not too much. Garnish with chopped onion and cheddar cheese. Serve with tortilla chips or corn bread.
Serves 8-10*

Curried Carrot & Rice

A wonderfully tasty and flavorful vegetarian dish.

Cook rice for about 25-30 minutes, until fluffy:	1/3 cup white rice 2/3 cup water
Reduce heat and add vegetable base and green curry paste:	2/3 tsp. vegetable base 2/3 tsp. green curry paste
In separate pot, cook carrots, bell peppers, ginger and sun-dried tomatoes until veggies are tender:	1 lg. carrot, diced 1/2 green bell pepper, diced 1/2 red bell pepper, diced 1/4 cup sun-dried tomatoes, chopped 1 tsp. minced ginger
In food processor, blend rice mixture & veggie mixture to make a smooth puree. Return to pot & add curry powder, salt, garlic, thyme, and coconut milk.	1 tsp. curry powder 2/3 tsp. granulated garlic 2/3 tsp salt Pinch of thyme 3/4 cup coconut milk

Heat to 160°.
Garnish with a sprig of parsley

Multi Veggie Chili

A delicious veggie-intensive meatless chili from a health-foods freak. It also makes a great salsa!

Spray nonstick dutch oven or large skillet with nonstick cooking spray. Heat over medium high heat until hot. Cook 5 minutes, stirring frequently.

1 cup chopped green bell peppers
1 cup chopped celery
1 cup chopped onion
3 cloves garlic, minced

Stir in, bring to a boil. Reduce heat, simmer uncovered 8-10 minutes or until celery is crisp-tender and flavors are blended, stirring occasionally:

1 (15 oz.) can tomato sauce
1 (15 1/2 oz.) can pinto beans, drained & rinsed
1 cup frozen whole kernel corn (or zucchini)
1 1/4 cups water
2 tsp. chili powder
1 tsp. dried oregano

Serves 4

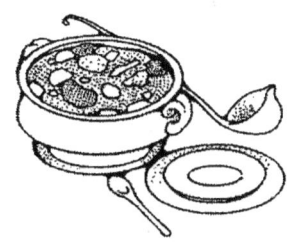

Turkey Vatapa

*An unusual and different dish,
good enough to set before
the Queen (or King).*

Heat oil in pot over medium-high heat. Add onions, garlic and sauté:

- 1 tsp. olive oil
- 1/2 cup chopped onion
- 2 tsp. minced garlic

Add jalapenos and ginger and sauté. Add tomatoes, water and beer and bring to boil. Cover and reduce heat; let simmer for 20 minutes:

- 1 tbsp. fresh ginger, minced
- 1 jalapeno pepper, minced
- 1 cup water
- 1 (28 oz.) can diced tomatoes, undrained
- 1 (12 oz.) can light beer

Grind peanuts in food processor until finely chopped. Add to pot along with turkey and coconut milk:

- 1/4 cup dry unsalted peanuts
- 3 cups diced turkey
- 1/2 cup coconut milk

Turn up heat, simmer for 5 minutes. Stir in parsley, cilantro, lime juice, salt and pepper:

- 1/3 cup parsley, finely chopped
- 1/3 cup cilantro, finely chopped
- 1 tbsp. lime juice
- 1 tsp. salt
- 1 tsp. black pepper

*Garnish with cilantro or lime slices.
Serves 4-6.*

Greek Meat Sauce

Pickling spices and cinnamon provide an added touch to this aromatic sauce. It's good tossed with almost any Greek or Italian (or American) dish any time you want a meat sauce with the touch of the exotic.

In a wide frying pan, cook onions in butter, over medium high heat until onions are limp. Transfer to Dutch oven or 8-qt. pan:	6 large onions, finely chopped 4 tbsp. butter
In the frying pan, brown meat in 4 portions, adding butter as needed for each portion:	6 lbs. lean ground beef 4 tbsp. butter
Add meat to onions. Place garlic, cinnamon sticks and pickling spices in a cheesecloth bag for easy removal:	3 cloves garlic, minced or pressed 2 sticks cinnamon 1 tbsp. whole mixed pickling spice
Add to meat and onion mixture along with tomato paste, salt, pepper to taste, and water:	6 (6 oz.) cans tomato paste 2 tbsp. salt Freshly ground pepper 1 quart water

Cover and simmer, stirring occasionally, for 3 hours or until flavors are blended and sauce has thickened. Makes 4 quarts. Freeze in smaller portions to use as needed.

Eat what you want

The Japanese eat very little fat and suffer fewer heart attacks than the British or Americans.

On the other hand, the French eat a lot of fat and also suffer fewer heart attacks than the British or Americans.

The Japanese drink very little red wine and suffer fewer heart attacks than the British or Americans.

The Italians drink excessive amounts of red wine, and also suffer fewer heart attacks than the British or Americans

> Conclusion: Eat and drink what you like. It's speaking English that kills you.

Broccoli Cheddar Pot Pie

A rich and flavorful pot pie with a Parmesan Biscuit Topping.

Microwave on high until potatoes are soft; place into large bowl:	2 lg. potatoes cut in small cubes 1/2 cup butter 1 lg. onion, chopped 2 carrots, peeled & diced 3 celery stalks, sliced 1/4 cup sherry 2 tbsp. minced garlic
Microwave for 3 minutes, or until it can be blended together. Pour mixture over the vegetables.	3 cups milk 1 cup grated cheddar or processed cheese spread
Add to vegetable mixture and mix thoroughly.	50 oz. of canned cream of potato soup 1 cup cheddar cheese, shredded 3 cups chopped broccoli If using frozen, thaw first 1/4 tsp. white pepper 1/3 tbsp. garlic powder

Scoop 1 1/2 cups of mixture into oven proof soup bowls. Top with parmesan biscuit rounds (recipe on next page). Brush with egg white. Bake at 350° for 20-25 minutes until bubbly and golden brown. Makes 6 large pot pies.

For a Chicken Pot Pie, use 3 1/2 cups cooked, diced chicken for broccoli, add 1/8 tsp. sage and 1/4 tsp. rosemary.

Pot Pie Parmesan Biscuit Topping

Yummy! Makes 6 large pot pie toppings.

Mix on low speed of mixer just until blended:	2 cups flour 1 tbsp. baking powder 1 tsp. sugar 1/2 tsp. salt 1/2 tsp. pepper 1/2 tsp. paprika 1/2 cup parmesan shredded 2 tbsp. chopped green onions
Add butter pieces and mix until coarse.	1/3 cup unsalted butter cut into 1/2 inch pieces
Blend in milk:	3/4 cup milk

Turn out onto a floured board and knead until the dough is no longer too sticky to work with.
Roll out dough to 1/4" thick.
Cut dough with paring knife, tracing around top of an upside down soup bowl.
Place biscuit rounds on the filled bowls.
Brush tops with egg whites.
Bake at 350° for 20-25 minutes until pot pies are bubbly and golden brown.

Colophon Pie Crust

*For use with recipes for quiche or fruit pies.
These tasty dishes are among the
Colophon customers' favorites!*

Blend in food processor for 10 seconds—no more. Mixture should be a course meal:

1/2 lb. unsalted butter, cubed
2 1/2 cups white flour
1 tsp. salt
2 tsp. sugar

Add slowly to running food processor. Blend until mixture just holds together. No longer than 30 seconds.

1/4 to 1/2 cup ice water

*Turn dough out onto pastry cloth. Divide in thirds
and pat into disks. Do not overwork this dough!
Wrap in parchment and refrigerate
for at least one hour.
Flour a pastry cloth and roll dough from
the center to the edge, turning pastry cloth and
adding flour as necessary.
When fitting into pie pan, allow about
1 1/2" extra dough.*

*Makes 3 crusts.
Crusts may be frozen after fitting into pie pan
if they are wrapped well.*

Pesto Quiche

Traditional egg pie with an Italian touch.

In unbaked 9" pie shell, layer half the mozzarella, the pesto, the sun-dried tomatoes and the rest of the cheese:

- 1 pie shell
- 3/4 cup ready-made pesto
- 1/2 cup sun-dried tomatoes
- 2 cups shredded mozzarella

Blend together:

- 4 eggs
- 1 1/2 cups milk

Pour batter over top of tomato/cheese mixture. Bake at 400° for 10 minutes, or until crust is lightly browned.
Reduce temperature to 300° and bake until quiche is set and knife comes out clean.

Quiche may be made out of almost anything! Simply fill a pie shell with three cups of ingredients—meats, cheeses, or vegetables—and then pour egg mixture over the top.

For added flavor on many quiches, add 1/4 tsp. dry hot mustard, and 1/4 tsp. cayenne pepper or a dash ground black pepper to the egg mixture.

Makes one Quiche

TexMex Haystack

*This recipe comes from one of our customers.
Try it, you'll like it!*

Mix together:	1 (16 oz.) can refried beans 1 can bean dip Garlic powder to taste 1/4 cup thick Picante sauce
Spread into 10x10 inch or 9x13 inch pan. Mash:	4 avocados with small amount of lemon juice 2 tbsp. guacamole mix
Spread over bean layer. Then spread over avocados:	1 pint sour cream
Have on hand to dice, then mix enough together to make a third layer:	Green onion Tomatoes Black olives Lettuce.

Top with grated mild cheese.
Serve with corn or flour tortilla chips.

To expand the dish, add another can refried beans, plus a little more salsa. If you can't get ripe avocados, use frozen guacamole.

"This is the dressing which I have made!" the emperor declared. "It shall be known as Caesar's"

From "The Idiots of March"
by Mama Colophon

Colophon Caesar Dressing

Several Colophon Chefs contributed their best home Caesars to this dressing. We make it without eggs.

In a shaker bottle add, then shake to mix. Refrigerate.
- 1/2 cup olive oil
- 5 cloves pressed or minced garlic
- 1 tbsp. lemon juice
- 2 tsp. Worchestershire Sauce
- 1 tsp. Dijon Mustard
- Freshly ground pepper

Toss together in a large bowl:
- Lettuce
- Grated parmesan cheese
- Homemade croutons

Shake well before pouring over salad! Serve with french bread.

For variations on this, add shrimp, smoked salmon or avocado to the salad!

Honey Sesame Dressing

A great dressing with an oriental flair.

In food processor or blender combine:	1/4 cup chopped onion 1 tsp fresh chopped ginger root
Add:	2/3 cup honey (softened in microwave)
Mix in mixer:	2 cups safflower oil 1 cup cider vinegar
To mixer add:	1 tsp. soy sauce 1/2 tsp. salt 1 tsp. paprika 1/2 tsp. dry mustard powder
Add food processor mixture to oil and vinegar in mixer. Then add:	1/3 cup toasted sesame seeds

If you need to toast the seeds, spread on a cookie sheet and bake at 350° 20-25 minutes until light brown.
Mix all together and refrigerate.

Shake well before serving!

Fat-Free Italian Artichoke Dressing

A "good" fat-free dressing is such an unusual thing, that when "Gourmet Magazine" discovered we had one, they wrote and requested our recipe!

Chop in food processor:	1 cup artichoke hearts, packed in water and drained
In mixer add:	1/4 cup chopped onion 1/2 cup apple cider vinegar 1 cup water 1/2 cup apple juice concentrate 1/4 cup minced garlic 1/8 cup honey 2 tsp. basil 2 tsp. oregano 1/2 tsp. white pepper

Mix in artichoke hearts and refrigerate. Shake well before serving!

Although the tomato is botanically a fruit, the U. S. Supreme Court in 1893 ruled the tomato to be legally a vegetable because it is ". . . usually served at dinner, in, with, or after the soup, fish or meat, which constitutes the principal part of the repast, and not, like fruits, generally as a dessert."

Jack's Cornet Bay Salad

This attractive but simple salad comes to us from a man who loves cooking as much, or more, than he loves the graphics business.

Slice into six segments. Press segments gently to form a cup: 4 firm tomatoes

Chop fine:
Mix vegetables with dressing and place in tomato cup.
1 cucumber
1/2 stalk celery
1/4 red pepper

Mix together for dressing:
1 cup mayonnaise
Capful lemon juice
1/4 cup pickle juice
1 tbsp. sugar
1/4 cup catsup
1/4 cup relish

Top with crab or shrimp.
Chill before serving.
Makes 4 servings.

Spinach Salad

*Recipe is from Catrina's Restaurant in Hayward, California.
We get around, don't we?*

Clean, wash and dry the spinach. Chill well.	2 bunches spinach
Trim bacon of excess fat. Sauté the bacon over medium heat until soft, not crisp.	4 slices lean bacon
Add to bacon:	1 tbsp. Worchestershire Sauce 1 tbsp. Dijon style mustard 1/4 cup red wine vinegar 1/4 cup sugar

*Stir and heat through.
Pour over spinach and toss well.
Serve with freshly ground pepper*

Hummus

An exotic blend of healthy stuff that tastes great on bagels, as a vegetable dip, or on vegetarian sandwiches.

Purée in food processor for 3 to 4 minutes:
- 4 cups cooked, drained garbanzo beans
- 2 tsp. cumin
- 2 tsp. salt
- 1/2 cup minced garlic
- 1 cup olive oil

Add:
- 1 (15 oz.) can or jar of Tahini (ground sesame seeds)
- 1 3/4 cups lemon juice

Blend in food processor until thoroughly mixed, then refrigerate.

Makes approximately 4 cups of Hummus

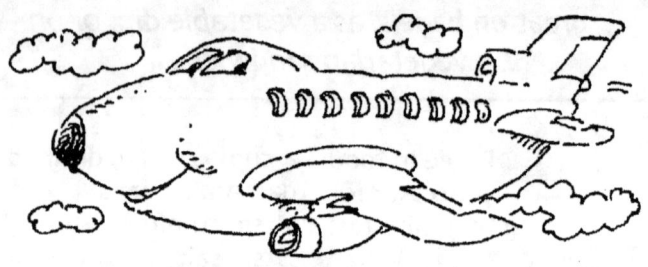

"Boss, de plane!" he cried, heading for the landing strip and the shipment of decadent desserts, which surely must have arrived.

From "Fantasy Food Island"
by Mama Colophon

Desserts, etc.

Desserts is just stressed spelled backwards!

Colophon Chocolate Chunk Cake

One of our most requested decadent dessert recipes, this one keeps them coming back!

Whisk together and set aside:	2/3 cup cocoa 1 cup boiling water
Cream together, then add the cocoa mixture:	3/4 cup butter 1 1/4 cup brown sugar 2/3 cup white sugar 2 eggs 1 egg yolk 1 tbsp. vanilla
Blend together and mix on high speed for 30 seconds:	3 cups white flour 1/2 tsp. salt 2 tsp. baking soda
Add slowly, mix on medium speed, scraping bowl often, for 30 seconds:	1 2/3 cups buttermilk

Pour batter into greased and floured 10 in. cake pan and bake at 350° until knife inserted comes out clean. Cook thoroughly and frost with Chocolate Frosting.

Makes one layer cake

Colophon Chocolate Frosting

Very rich, creamy frosting for Chocolate Chunk Cake or any other homemade goodies.

Cream together:	1 cup soft butter 1 1/2 cups cocoa powder
Add and mix well:	3 1/2 cups powdered sugar
Add very slowly to mixer:	1/2 cup Half & Half

Mix all together on high for 15 seconds, scraping bowl thoroughly.

Frost cake and garnish top with whole milk chocolate chips or grated chocolate and nuts if desired.

Frosts one layer cake

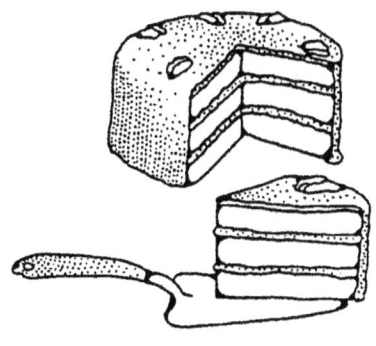

Colophon Peanut Butter Pie

This pie is so delicious, "Bon Appetit" requested our recipe and printed it in the August, 1993 issue. This recipe is a 2 pager, and makes 2 pies.

Mix together in a large bowl and set aside:
1 (8 oz.) cream cheese
1 1/2 cups crunchy peanut butter
1 1/2 cups brown sugar
1 tsp. vanilla

Whip on low speed for two minutes:
2 cups heavy whipping cream

Add and whip on high speed until peaks form (do NOT overwhip or cream will turn buttery!):
1/2 cup powdered sugar

Fold the whipped cream mixture into the peanut butter mixture. Divide mixture into two 8 inch Chocolate Cookie Crusts. Spread evenly and freeze pies for 3 hours.
(Recipe continued on next page.)

Colophon Peanut Butter Pie Continued
And the cookie crust to bake them in!

Melt in separate bowl in the microwave for 30-45 seconds. Stir until smooth

2 cups melting chocolate (or semisweet chocolate chips)
1/2 cup Half & Half

Pie topping: Carefully spoon half the chocolate ganache on the top of each frozen pie. Spread evenly and quickly garnish with 1 tbsp. chopped peanuts before the chocolate sets. Chill for 1 hour before cutting. Use a knife dipped in hot water for cutting.

This recipe makes two pies.
They may be frozen for storage.
To thaw, place in refrigerator for several hours.
They will cut more easily if partially frozen.

Chocolate Cookie Crust
For the Colophon Peanut Butter Pie

Combine well by hand or food processor
4 1/2 cups finely ground chocolate cookie crumbs
and 1/2 cup butter melted
Divide in half and press into two pie tins.
Bake 7-10 minutes at 350°

Cookies!

*Wonder just who fashioned the first cookie,
and under what circumstance.
Perhaps some stone-age mother robbed a bee's
nest for honey, spread it on a leftover piece of
dough made from stone-ground wheat or
barley, and baked it over the flowing coals of
the morning fire after the family
had finished off breakfast.
Back then it was "waste not, want not,"
much as it should continue to be.
And lo! The cookie was born!*

Dave's Breakfast Cookies

Low-Fat cookies make great tasting healthful snacks.

Mix together in mixing bowl:	1 1/2 cups applesauce 1 1/8 cups brown sugar 1/2 cup apple juice 1/6 cup orange juice 1/6 cup lemon juice 2 tbsp. vanilla
Mix in:	1 mashed banana
Stir in:	3/4 cup flour 1/2 cup wheat flour 1 tbsp. baking soda 1/2 tbsp. cinnamon 1/2 tbsp. nutmeg 1/2 tbsp. ginger 3/4 tsp. cloves
Stir in:	4 cups oats 2 cups Rice Krispies 3/4 cup crushed cornflakes 3/4 cups dried fruit

These cookies are very moist. It is easiest to use an ice cream scoop and drop the dough on a parchment lined cookies sheet. Dip fingers into water and pat cookies into flat circles. Bake at 325° 12-15 minutes. They will not spread while baking. Makes 24 cookies

Colophon Cookies

One of our hottest selling cookies.

Cream together: 1 cup butter
1 cup brown sugar
1/2 cup white sugar

Add and mix: 2 eggs
1/2 tbsp. vanilla

Add: 2 cups white flour
1 tsp. baking powder
1 tsp. baking soda
1/2 tsp. salt

Add: 1 3/4 cups oats
1 1/2 cups Rice Krispies
3/4 cup white choc chips
3/4 cup butterscotch chips
3/4 cup pecans

Drop batter onto nonstick cookie sheet.
Bake at 350" until golden
Makes 20 medium or 10 giant cookies

Hey diddle diddle
I've a bulge in my middle
I hope to whittle it soon.
But eating's such fun,
I won't get it done,
'Til my dish runs away
 with my spoon!   D. Neil

Bapple Cookies

Like "trail mix" in a cookie, many people eat just these instead of a full lunch!

Cream together in a large bowl:	3/4 cup butter 3/4 cup white sugar 1/2 cup brown sugar 3 eggs, add one at a time
Add:	3/4 tsp. vanilla 1/2 cup apple juice 1/8 cup cooled espresso
Mix together:	2 1/2 cups flour 2 tsp. baking soda 1/2 tsp. salt 1/2 tsp. allspice 1/2 tsp. nutmeg 2 tsp. cinnamon 3 3/4 cups oats
Stir in and mix well, scraping sides and bottom of bowl:	1 med. chopped apple 3/4 cup raisins 3/4 cup chocolate chips 1/2 cup chopped walnuts

Drop rounded spoonfuls of dough onto parchment lined cookie sheet. Dip fingers in cold water and press cookies into round, flat patties. They will not spread. Sprinkle each with 1/2 tsp. chopped walnuts. Bake at 325° 10-12 min. or until light to med brown. Do not overcook! Makes about 2 dozen large cookies

A Fat Cat

A cat is good for catching mice,
A horse is good for hauling,
A pig is good to roast and slice,
A calf is good for bawling.

A frog has most expensive legs,
A ram is good for mutton,
A hen is good for laying eggs,
A squirrel is good for nuttin'!

Low Fat Muffins

*Health Clubs buy these from us.
They taste too good to be low fat!*

Mix on high speed for one minute to break up whites:	1 cup sugar 5 egg whites
Add and mix:	2 teaspoons vanilla 3/4 cup applesauce 1/2 cup nonfat sour cream 1 cup buttermilk
Combine and add to wet mixture. Do not overmix!	3 3/4 cup white flour 1 1/2 tbsp. baking powder 1 tsp. baking soda 1/2 tsp. salt
Stir into flour mixture:	1 cup fresh or frozen fruit

*Fill paper muffin cups.
Sprinkle lightly with sugar.
Bake at 325° for 15 minutes or until pick comes out clean.*

Makes 8 large muffins

Peanut Butter Fantasies

Decadently special dessert bars. Wonderful!

Cream together:	3/4 cup butter 3/4 cup brown sugar 1 egg 1/2 tsp. vanilla
Add and mix:	3/4 cup wheat flour 3/4 cup white flour 1/2 tsp. baking powder 1/4 tsp. baking soda 1/4 tsp. salt
Press mixture. Bake at 325° for 15 minutes, or until crust is lightly browned:	Dip fingers in water and press mixture into greased and floured 9X13 inch pan.
Cream together and spread over top of crust:	1/2 cup butter 2 cups crunchy peanut butter 1/2 teaspoon vanilla 1 cup powdered sugar
Sprinkle on top of peanut butter:	1 1/2 cups semisweet chocolate chips

Bake pan in 325° oven for 1 to 2 minutes to melt chocolate.
Garnish with toasted coconut. Chill before cutting.

The Yogi's Banana Bread

*Discovered in the 70's
by a Yogi in Bellingham.*

Mix in food processor:	1 cup brown sugar 1/2 cup softened butter 2 eggs 3 or 4 very ripe bananas
Add to food processor and blend thoroughly:	2 cups flour 1 tsp. baking powder 1/2 tsp. salt 1/2 tsp. baking soda 1 tsp. cinnamon 1 tsp. cloves 1 tsp. nutmeg
Add to food processor and blend very lightly:	1 cup frozen blueberries 1 cup chopped cashews

Bake in well greased loaf pan at 325° for about 1 hour. Test with a knife to see if it's done in the middle. Remove from pan and set on wire rack to cool.
Slice and serve.

Marge Starks, the creator of "Old Marge's Cheesecake," is a great musician and a great human being. A Seattle pianist, Marge has released several recordings of her standards, and show tunes from the 1930s to now, to benefit "Rosehedge," an assisted living residence for AIDS patients in Seattle.

Old Marge's Cheesecake

Marge's son Jim taught us how to make this divinely rich cheesecake while we were in college. He once sold them to restaurants in Cannon Beach, Oregon.

Mix in food processor and press mixture into bottom of glass pie pan to form a crust. Bake crust 10 minutes at 375°:

1 pkg. (1/4 lb.) graham crackers, crushed
3/4 melted stick of butter
1/4 cup sugar

In mixer, blend until smooth & pour into crust. Bake again for 20 minutes:

2 (8 oz.) packages softened cream cheese
2 eggs
1/2 cup sugar
1 tsp. vanilla

Mix by hand:

1 cup sour cream
1/2 tsp. vanilla
1/2 tsp lemon juice
2 tbsp. sugar

Pour mixture over pie and smooth with knife or spatula. Bake again for five minutes. Remove from oven, cool and refrigerate. Serve very cold as is, or with berries on top.

Makes one pie.

Apple Crisp

A dessert that combines basic apple and oatmeal goodness is sure to be loved by all. Sweet enough for the young, it also complements an after-dinner cup of coffee.

Spread thinly sliced apples over the bottom of a greased 8x8x2-inch baking dish.

4 or 5 medium-size tart cooking apples, cored peeled, & sliced thinly

In a mixing bowl, combine the brown sugar, granulated sugar, flour and oats, then stir in the melted butter:

6 tbsp. firmly packed light brown sugar
6 tbsp. granulated sugar
1/2 cup unsifted all-purpose flour
3/4 cup uncooked quick-cooking rolled oats
1/2 cup (1 stick) butter, melted

Spread mixture over the apples. Pour the water evenly over the top.

1/2 cup water

Bake, uncovered, in 375° preheated oven, until apples are tender, about 30 minutes. Serve warm or at room temperature with whipped cream or ice cream, if desired.
Serves 4.

Almond-Vanilla Apples

This recipe is a bit unusual, and comes to us from that other coast, even though it uses our wonderful Washington apples.

Peel, core & thinly slice apples. Toss with lemon juice to coat. Butter a 1 1/2 qt. baking dish and spread apples over the bottom:	2 1/2 lbs. tart cooking apples 1 1/2 tbsp. fresh lemon juice
Sift together flour, sugar, salt and cinnamon. Stir in almonds:	1 cup sifted flour 1 1/2 cups sugar 1/4 tsp. salt 1/4 tsp. cinnamon 2/3 cup almonds, finely chopped
Mix the melted butter with the vanilla:	1/2 cup unsalted butter, melted 1 tsp. vanilla extract

Add almond-flour mixture and toss with fork until mixed and crumbly. Sprinkle evenly over apples. Bake at 375° un til topping is richly browned, about 35-40 minutes. Can be made ahead.
Serve with softly whipped cream. Serves 6.

Colophon's Best Recipes
Alphabetical Index

African Peanut, The Original 9
Almond-Vanilla Apples 69
Apple Crisp 68
Banana Bread, The Yogi's 65
Broccoli Cheddar Chowder 16
Broccoli Cheddar Pot Pie 39
Broccoli, Cream of 15
Cheesecake, Old Marge's 67
Chili, Multi Vegetable 35
Chocolate Chunk Cake......... 54
Chocolate Frosting 55
Chocolate Cookie Crust 57
Clam Chowder, Manhattan 17
Colophon Caesar Dressing, ... 45
Cookies, Bapple 61
Cookies, Colophon 60
Cookies, Dave's 59
Croutons, Colophon 11
Curried Carrot & Rice 34
Curried Corn & Cheddar Chowder .20
Dressing, Fat-Free Artichoke .. 47
Dressing, Honey Sesame 46
Dutch Tomato Gouda 25
Gazpacho..................... 19
Greek Meat Sauce 37
Hummus 51

Mexican Corn & Bean Sopa ... 13
Muffins, Low-Fat 63
Peanut Butter Fantasies 64
Peanut Butter Pie 56
Pie Crust, Colophon 41
Pollo Tortilla Soupa 22
Pot Pie Biscuit Topping 40
Quiche. Pesto 42
Red Pepper Cheddar Soup 26
Salad, Jack's Cornet Bay 49
Salad, Spinach................ 50
Salmon Dill Bisque 23
Spicy Moroccan Bean 27
Split Pea Soup 11
Sweet Potato Bisque 29
TexMex Haystack 43
Thai Ginger Chicken Soup 21
Tomato Parmesan 14
Turkey Chili, Ray's 33
Turkey Vatapa 36

70

A BIG THANK YOU to all Colophon staff, past and present, who contributed their culinary knowledge and special recipes to the Colophon Cafe. Thanks also to our many customers around the world, whose thoughtful comments and appreciative palates made this book possible.

MAMA COLOPHON
(our founder)

Notes

Mama Colophon

Best Soups
of
The Colophon Cafe
Fairhaven, Washington

A Stirring Plot for Cooking Pots,
starring
Quality, Service, Consistency, and Cleanliness!

1208 11th Street (Fairhaven)
Bellingham, Washington 98225
360-647-0092

For more recipes and information, log on to ColophonCafe.com

First published by Mama Colophon, Inc. 1996.
Revised 2007, 2011.
This facsimile edition published by Chuckanut Editions, 2012.

These recipes may be reproduced for personal use only.

The who, what, when, where and why of Fairhaven

In 1858, because of the gold strikes in British Columbia, Fort Bellingham, located on what was then Whatcom Bay, found itself the center of about 15,000 people, and the Bay was clogged with ships.

During that manic time, Whatcom Bay was the most convenient port to get goods from the U.S. to Canada's Fort Langley and the Fraser River.

In 1883, a man named Dan Harris, having made his own gold strike by selling rice, vegetables, hardware and hard liquor out of a sloop in Whatcom Bay, bought a claim south of the towns of Whatcom and Bellingham.

Hoping to attract eastern investors, Harris named his claim Fairhaven, built a hotel and began to offer lots for gold. By 1885 he had done well enough to move to Los Angeles!

The real-estate boom of 1888 and 1889 brought Nelson Bennet, a wealthy developer to the area. He brought railroads into town, connecting Fairhaven with Whatcom to the north and with the main line between Vancouver, B.C. and Vancouver, Wash.

Another Californian, Jim Wardner, organized the Fairhaven Water Works Co., the Fairhaven Electric Light Co., the Samish Lake Logging & Milling Co., the Cascade Club and two banks. His 23-room "mansion," Wardner's Castle, is on the historical register.

The Depression of 1893 ended the Fairhaven boom. But coal mines, timber and shipping kept the towns of Whatcom and Fairhaven (which included the old town of Bellingham) going, and in 1904 they merged into a single city, Bellingham.

Taken from Paul Dorpat's "Now and Then," and from the Whatcom County Centennial Committee.

What does it all mean?

COLOPHON: (kol'e fon')

1. A publishers distinctive emblem.

2. An inscription at the end of a book, usually with facts relative to its publication.

3. Greek koloph'on: summit, finishing touch, the last word.

4. The Colophon Cafe is the last word in good eating.

5. Pronounced "Call-a-fawn" Cafe

Mama Colophon

Contents

Chowders
Clam Chowder 8
Vegan Corn Chowder 9
Curried Corn & Cheddar 10
Manhattan Clam Chowder 11

Chilies
Corn Chili 14
Lentil Chili 15
Black Bean Chili 16
Rays Turkey Chili 17

Cream Soups
Cream of Almond 20
Cream of Broccoli 21
Asparagus Bisque 22
Cream of Dill Pickle 23
Turkey Almondine 24
Cream of Mushroom 25
Cream of Chicken Mushroom 26
Cream of Spinach 27

Cold Weather Soups
Cheddar Ale (Beer Cheese) 31
Lemon Chicken Rice 32
Butter Bean Dijon 33
Kielbasa Bean 34
Pumpkin Almond 35
Turkey Rice 36
Tomato Cheddar 37
Cauliflower Cheddar 38
Tomato Rice 39
Barbecue Ham 40
Tomato Parmesan 41

Vegetarian Soups

Christmas Corn 44
Gazpacho 45
Italian Barley 46
Mexican Corn & Bean 47
Colophon Croutons 48
Split Pea 49
Three Sisters 51
Green Onion Potato Dill 52
Vegetarian Vegetable 53
Tomato Florentine 54
Potato Leek 55
Colophon Cabbage 57

Exotic Soups

The Original African Peanut 61
Spicy Thai Rice 62
Colophon Carrot 63
Mediterranean Vegetable 64
Jamaican Red Bean 65
Curried Turkey & Apple .66
Avgolemono 67
Curried Banana 68
Thai Ginger Chicken 69

Alphabetical Index on page 70.

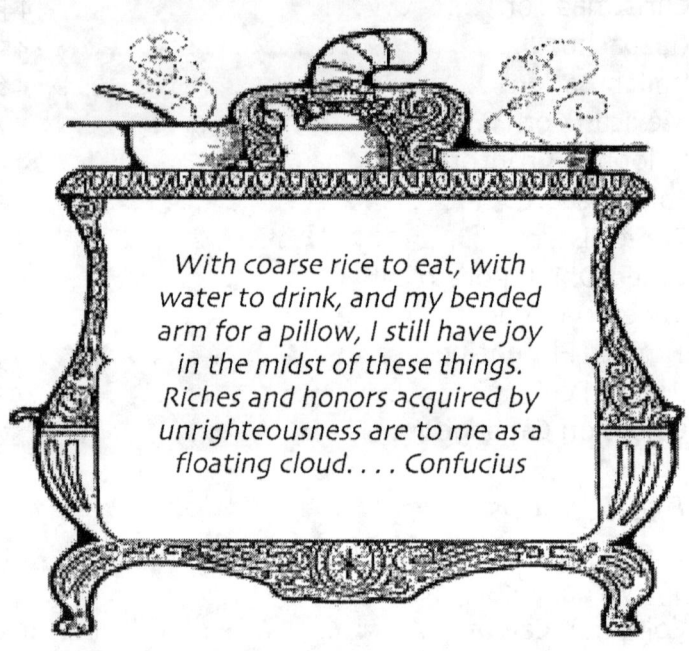

With coarse rice to eat, with water to drink, and my bended arm for a pillow, I still have joy in the midst of these things. Riches and honors acquired by unrighteousness are to me as a floating cloud. . . . Confucius

Clam Chowder

The Colophon Cafe's original "Crowded Clam Chowder" Don't hesitate to add scallops, shrimp, prawns, or fish to this wonderful chowder!

Sauté in large soup pot till onions are tender:
- 1 tbsp. butter
- 1 medium onion, diced
- 2 cloves minced garlic

Combine and cook until potatoes are done:
- 30 oz. clam juice
- 30 oz. water (or cover potatoes)
- 1 1/2 lbs. potatoes, cubed
- 1 medium carrot, diced
- 1/4 cup dried potatoes
- 1 tsp. parsley
- 1 tsp. thyme
- 1 tsp. tarragon
- Salt & pepper to taste

Once potatoes are cooked, make a Roux paste and add to thicken:
- Roux: 1/4 cup melted butter and 1/4 cup flour

Finally, add and simmer: DO NOT BOIL!
- 1 pint Half & Half
- 1 lb. chopped clams

Hints: In separate pot, ladle some juice from soup and whisk in warm Roux – then add to soup to thicken. Thin with Half & Half and then add seafood. Thin with additional warmed whole milk if needed. Garnish with goldfish crackers.
Serves 6-8

Vegan Corn Chowder

A non dairy, low calorie chowder, perfect as a first course, or main course served with corn bread and honey

---

Cook 30 minutes, or until mushy, in just enough water to cover the veggies:
- 2 or 3 cubed potatoes
- 1 chopped onion
- 1 chopped carrot
- 1 stalk chopped celery

Add to soup pot with:
- 1/2 lb. bag frozen corn
- 1 (15 oz.) can creamed corn

Heat to 160 degrees, and serve.
- 1 tsp. garlic powder
- 1 tsp. salt
- 1 tsp. pepper
- 1/4 tsp. nutmeg
- Dash of Tabasco

Thin with soy milk to desired consistency.

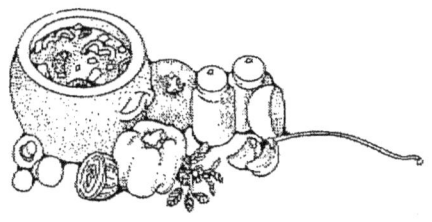

Garnish with parsley or tortilla chips.
Serves 4-6

Curried Corn & Cheddar Chowder

A mildly curried soup with the rich taste of cheddar and sweet corn.

Whip together in soup pot:	1 quart hot water 1 lb. cream cheese
Add, then heat to a slow boil:	1 (16 oz.) can creamed corn 4 tsp. curry powder 1 tsp. black pepper 1/2 cup chopped onion
Add, and heat to a slow boil:	1-1/2 lbs. frozen corn 2 stalks chopped celery
Add, reduce heat to a simmer:	Roux: 3 tbsp. flour mixed into 3 tbsp. melted butter
Add to soup and stir in gently:	1 cup cheddar cubes (cut the cheddar into 1/2 in. cubes and put them into a small bag with a couple of tablespoons flour, and shake it up}

Garnish with cheddar cheese,
grated or cut into shapes.
Serves 4-6

Manhattan Clam Chowder

For years the Colophon served only a white clam chowder, until we tasted this wonderful red version created by our soup chef. It's spicy, delicious and easy to make.

In soup pot, cook until potatoes are done, in just enough water to cover:

- 1 medium white onion, diced
- 3 small cubed potatoes
- 1 peeled carrot, diced
- Juice of 2 (6-1/2 oz.) cans chopped clams
- 1 (8 oz.) bottle clam juice
- 2 tbsp. parsley
- 1 red pepper, diced
- 2 tbsp. instant mashed potatoes
- 1 tsp. thyme
- 1 tsp. black pepper
- 1 tsp. salt

Add, heat to slow boil, then turn down to simmer for 10 minutes or so before serving.

- 1 (14-1/2 oz.) can diced tomatoes with juice
- 2 cups vegetable juice
- 2 cans of chopped clams (that were left from the juice you added)

Garnish with goldfish crackers.
Serves 4-6

"Dancing clams are fine for the big city, but have you seen our hoofing holsteins?

"Most definitely a two thumbs up kind of chili," he announced confidently, "and don't even think of putting any cow in it."

Corn Chili

A spicy, vegetarian chili, great served as a prelude to Mexican food, or as a meal in itself.
Serve with blue tortilla chips and bean dip on the side.

Saute in a little olive oil until tender.	1 medium onion, minced
Combine in soup pot and heat to 160 degrees:	1 (20 oz.) can creamed corn 2 (20 oz.) cans water 1/4 cup corn meal 2 tsp. chili powder 1/2 tsp. black pepper 1 tsp. cumin 1 tbsp. honey 1/4 cup green chilies, minced 1/2 cup red peppers, diced
Add, and heat to 160 degrees:	1 lb. bag frozen corn (fresh or canned also works)
Add, and stir in:	Roux: 3 tbsp. flour mixed into 3 tbsp. melted butter

Simmer for half an hour, stirring gently once in a while.

Garnish with tortilla chips or grated cheese.
Serves 4-6

Lentil Chili

This thick, vegetarian chili makes a great main meal served with pita bread wedges, hummus, and sliced cucumbers and tomatoes

---

Combine in soup pot, cover and cook until lentils are tender but firm:	2-1/2 cups water 1 cup lentils 1/2 cup pearl barley 1 red onion, minced 3 cloves garlic, minced
In small bowl, mix with hot water to a thin paste-like consistency, then add to soup pot:	3 tsp. chili powder 1 tsp. sugar 1 tsp. black pepper 2 tsp. cumin 2 tsp. vinegar 1 tsp. salt
When lentils are nearly done, add:	1 chopped carrot 2 stalks diced celery
When cooked, add and heat to 150 degrees:	1 (15 oz.) can diced tomatoes 2 cups vegetable juice

Thin with vegetable juice or water if needed, but keep it thick.

Garnish with a dollop of sour cream and a tortilla chip. Serve chips on the side.
Serves 4-6

Black Bean Chili

*Another great Mexican-style chili.
For an exotic dip, serve it with grated cheese
and corn tortilla chips*

Sauté in butter or olive oil until onions are translucent:	1 medium onion, chopped 4 cloves garlic, minced 1 carrot, chopped
Cook until beans are tender but not mush, takes a couple of hours:	1 lb. black beans, rinsed and cleaned 1 quart water
In small bowl, mix with water to a thin paste-like consistency:	3 tsp. chili powder 1 tsp. sugar 2 tsp. garlic powder 1 tsp. black pepper 2 tsp. cumin 2 tsp. vinegar 1 tsp. salt 3 tsp. lemon juice
Add to soup pot and simmer for 1/2 hour:	2 (15 oz.) cans diced tomatoes 16 oz. vegetable juice or tomato juice

*Garnish with a dollop of sour cream
Serves 4-6*

Ray's Turkey Chili

An amazing chili made without beef or beans! Reprinted from our "Best Recipes" cookbook. A perfect use for those Thanksgiving turkey leftovers

---

Heat oil in a large soup pot and add these, stirring until cooked:	3 tbsp. olive oil 1 red onion, chopped 1 yellow onion, chopped 2 leeks, chopped 6 cloves garlic, chopped
Mix these together, adding just enough of the beer to form a thin paste. Stir paste into cooked vegetables:	2 tbsp. flour 6 tbsp. chili powder 1 tbsp. oregano 1 tbsp. salt 2 tbsp. cumin powder 1 to 2 tsp. cayenne pepper Cold beer
Add and stir well:	3 lbs. cooked turkey, chopped 2 (14 –1/2 oz.) cans stewed tomatoes, with juice 1 (14 oz.) can tomato sauce 4-5 tbsp. of the beer (drink the rest!) 1 tbsp. peanut butter

Stir often and simmer on low heat 2-5 hours. Add beer or water to thin, but not too much.

Garnish with chopped onion and cheddar cheese.
Serve with tortilla chips or corn bread.
Serves 8-10

"The stalks were as high as a bovine's eye,
and the corn made her moo with pride."

Cream Soups

Cream of Almond Soup

Turkey or chicken may be added to this soup to make it winter hearty

---

Cook in soup pot until fluffy (about 20 minutes):	2 cups water 3/4 cup pearl rice
Mix together well. Add to soup pot and heat to 160 degrees:	1-1/2 cups chicken stock or consommé 1/2 tsp. almond extract 8 oz. water
Melt into soup and whip it smooth. Heat to 160 degrees:	1/4 lb. cream cheese
At 160 degrees, add Roux, and heat to 150 degrees and serve:	Roux: 3 tbsp. flour mixed into 3 tbsp. melted butter

Thin with milk if needed.
Garnish with sliced almonds.
Serves 4-6

Cream of Broccoli Soup

*A thick, rich, tasty cream soup
great with french bread.*

Sauté in soup pot:	1 tbsp. butter 1 medium onion, minced 3 cloves garlic, minced
Add, cover with water, and cook:	3/4 lb. thawed frozen broccoli, chopped
Reduce heat and add:	2 stalks celery, chopped 1/2 tsp. salt 1/2 tsp. pepper Squeeze of lemon Dash of Tabasco
In separate bowl, combine and whip until smooth, then add to soup pot and heat to 160 degrees:	1/4 lb softened cream cheese 1 cup warmed milk
At 160 degrees, add:	Roux: 3 tbsp. flour mixed into 3 tbsp. melted butter

Reduce heat to 145 degrees and thin with milk.

*Garnish with cheddar cheese wedge
or broccoli crowns.
Serves 8-10*

Asparagus Bisque

*Our preferred version of Cream of Asparagus
A creamy way to get your vegetables. Serve with
a meal of roast chicken and steamed potatoes.*

Sauté in soup pot until tender:	1 tbsp. butter 1 small onion, diced 3 cloves garlic, minced
Add to soup pot, cook until rice is done (about 20 minutes):	1/4 cup parboiled rice 1 cup water
Add the following and cook until asparagus is done:	2 lbs. asparagus, chopped 1/2 cup water 1 tsp. dill weed 1 tsp. tarragon 1/2 tsp. pepper 1 tsp. rosemary Dash of Tabasco
Strain out and puree in food processor:	Asparagus and rice
Add to thicken soup, continue to heat to 160 degrees:	Roux: 3 tbsp. flour mixed into 3 tbsp. melted butter 1/4 lb. cream cheese 1 cup whole milk

*Hints: After asparagus & rice are cooked, strain them and puree in food processor. Ladle some hot soup stock into a separate pot and whisk in the Roux. Add this to your final soup to thicken. Then add the cream cheese and thin with warm whole milk. Garnish soup with cheddar wedge.
Serves 6-8.*

Cream of Dill Pickle Soup

*A dear friend, heavy with child, laughingly asked,
"Why don't you ever have any soups with dill pickles in it?
The next day we served this as our featured soup.*

Cook until almost done, about 20 minutes:	1/2 cup pearl rice 1-1/2 cups water
Soften on hot rice:	1/4 lb. cream cheese
Add and stir:	1 quart hot water 1/2 tsp. dry mustard 1/2 tsp. thyme 1 tbsp. garlic powder Salt to taste
Add, then whip smooth:	8 oz. dill pickles, chopped fine 1/4 cup pickle juice
Heat to 150 degrees and stir in:	Roux: 3 tbsp. flour mixed into 3 tbsp. melted butter

*Garnish with fresh dill.
Serves 4-6.*

Turkey Almondine Soup

*A very rich, creamy soup best served before a meal.
Too exotic to serve with bread,
use flavored rice crackers.*

Cook in soup pot, until fluffy (about 20 minutes):	1 cup water 1 cup chicken stock or broth 3/4 cups rice
Add to soup pot:	1/2 tsp. almond extract 1/4 cup almonds, chopped 1/4 lb. cream cheese
Heat to 160 degrees:	1 medium carrot, chopped 1 tsp. garlic powder 1 tsp. thyme 1 tsp. sage 1 red bell pepper, chopped 1 green bell pepper, chopped
Add and simmer:	Roux: 3 tbsp. flour mixed into 3 tbsp. melted butter 1/2 lb. chopped, cooked turkey

*Thin with milk if needed
Garnish soup with sliced almonds.
Serves 4-6*

Cream of Mushroom Soup

You'll never buy canned again!

Cook until fluffy (about 20 minutes):	3 cups water 3/4 cup pearl rice
Soften on the hot rice, then whip smooth:	1/4 lb. cream cheese
Add and heat to 160 degrees:	1 quart water 1 tsp. dry mustard 1 tsp. nutmeg 1-1/2 lbs. sliced mushrooms 1 tsp. salt Dash of pepper to taste
Add and reheat to 150 degrees:	Roux: 3 tbsp. flour mixed into 3 tbsp. melted butter
Add and reheat to 150 degrees:	4 oz. Half & Half 2 oz. cream sherry 4 oz. milk

Garnish with mushroom slices.
Serves 4-6

Cream of Chicken Mushroom Soup

The best of two flavors in a thick, flavorful soup.

Cook in soup pot, until fluffy (about 20 minutes):
- 1/2 cup rice
- 1 cup water
- 2 cups chicken broth
- 1/4 onion, chopped
- 1 lb. sliced fresh mushrooms

Add to soup pot and heat to 160 degrees:
- 1/8 cup lemon juice
- 1 tsp. tarragon
- 1/2 tsp. thyme
- 1 tsp. garlic
- 1/2 tsp. dry mustard
- 1/2 tsp. nutmeg
- 1 tsp. salt
- Dash of black pepper

Combine in separate bowl until smooth, then add to pot, and heat to 160 degrees:
- 1/4 lb. cream cheese
- 1 cup steamed milk

Add to pot and simmer for awhile. DO NOT LET IT BOIL!
- Roux: 1 tbsp. flour mixed into 1 tbsp. melted butter

Garnish with slivered almonds.
Serves 4-8.

Cream of Spinach Soup
Popeye would have approved!

Cover with 2 cups water, bring to a slow boil, then simmer covered for about 20 minutes:
- 1-1/2 lbs. fresh or thawed frozen spinach
- 1 medium onion, minced
- 1 stalk celery, chopped
- 2 cloves garlic, minced
- 1 tsp. salt
- 1/2 tsp. pepper
- Squeeze of lemon
- Dash of Tabasco

In separate bowl, combine and whip until smooth, add to soup pot and heat to 160 degrees:
- 1/4 lb softened cream cheese
- 1 cup warmed milk

At 160 degrees, add:
- Roux: 3 tbsp. flour mixed into 3 tbsp. melted butter

Reduce heat to 145 degrees and thin with milk if needed

Garnish with cheddar cheese wedge.
Serves 4-6.

Soup is a welcome part of any meal, but cool days bring out the best in the Soup Elf.

The Soup Elf is that imaginary sprite that lurks in every good kitchen.

He wears a tiny black soup pot for a hat, and his hands are wee paddles for stirring.

He is never so happy as when he sits on the rim of the simmering soup pot inhaling the aromas of stock made with vegetables and with a dash of garlic and a splash of wine.

Cold Weather Soups

And during an unusually hot and sweltering St. Patrick's Day, the soft cheddar slipped from beneath the bun of his kielbasa, splashing into his warm beer, thus creating the first beer cheese soup.

Cheddar Ale Soup
(AKA Beer Cheese Soup)
One of the most requested soups at the Colophon, our version of beer cheese soup is thick and very rich. Serve it inside a hollowed out bread bowl!

Combine in soup pot and heat to 160 degrees:	24 oz. water 12 oz. beer or ale of your choice A generous dash of Tabasco 2 cloves garlic, minced 1/2 tsp. black pepper 1/2 tsp. thyme Pinch of salt
Add to thicken soup. Continue to heat to 160 degrees:	Roux: 3 tbsp. flour mixed into 3 tbsp. melted butter 12 oz. sharp cheddar cold pack cheese spread 2 oz. heavy whipping cream 1 oz. sliced black olives

Hints: Whisk warm Roux into soup to thicken.
Let cheddar pack spread warm to
room temperature,
then whisk into soup.
Add whipping cream to thin to your liking.

Garnish with popcorn and serve with sliced French Bagette.
Serves 4-6

Lemon Chicken Rice Soup

This tangy lemon soup would make any Grandma proud.

Bring water and chicken broth to a boil. Add rice and simmer, covered, for 20 minutes, or until rice is done:
- 1 cup rice
- 3/4 cups water
- 1 cup chicken broth

Add to soup pot. Heat to slow boil, then turn heat down. Simmer for about 30 minutes:
- 1-1/2 cups cooked, diced chicken
- 1/4 cup lemon juice
- 1 tsp. salt
- 1 tsp. pepper
- Dash of Tabasco
- 1 small carrot, diced fine
- 1 cup frozen peas
- 2 cups water
- 2 cups chicken broth

Garnish with paper-thin slice of lemon. Serves 4-6.

"Noise proves nothing. Often a hen who has merely laid an egg cackles as if she had laid an asteroid"
. . . Mark Twain

Butter Bean Dijon Soup

*A simple to make soup that tastes great on a cold day.
Just put it in the pot and let it cook!*

Add all ingredients to large soup pot:
- 1 lb. butter or baby lima beans
- 1 medium carrot, chopped
- 1/2 lb. ham, diced
- 3 tbsp. dijon mustard
- 2 cloves garlic, minced
- 1/2 tsp. pepper
- 1/2 tsp. salt

This soup needs to simmer for at least a couple of hours, until the beans are tender.

Garnish with a drizzle of dijon mustard.
Serves 4-6

The shiny black Rolls pulled to a stop beside the psychedelic VW bus. " Do you have any Butter Bean Dijon?" inquired the wealthy occupant. In silent response, an arm extended, handing him a Colophon Cafe Soup Calendar.

Kielbasa Bean Soup

*Hearty with a sandwich at lunch or as an entree for dinner.
This soup may be garnished with cheddar cheese
and served with a thick french bread*

Saute with olive oil in soup pot until tender:	1 medium onion, chopped 1 carrot, chopped 3 cloves of garlic, chopped
Add all ingredients. Cook until done. Serve at 150 degrees:	1/4 lb. black eyed peas 1/4 lb. great northern beans 1/4 lb. small white beans 1/4 lb. small red beans 1/4 lb. pinto beans 2-1/2 cups water 1/2 tsp. thyme 1/2 tsp. marjoram 1/2 tsp. pepper 1/2 tsp. salt
	1 lb kielbasa sausage cut into 1/8 inch slices

Garnish with a thin slice of
keilbasa, or fresh parsley.

*To do two things at once is to do neither . . .
Publilius Syrus in 1st Century BC.
To eat two things at once is to do lunch . . .
Mama Colophon, 21st Century AD.*

Pumpkin Almond Soup

This is a great soup to serve to kids in a hollowed out pumpkin. You can paint a jack-o-lantern face on the outside with felt-tip markers.

Heat and whip:	3 cups hot water 1/4 lb. cream cheese (lowfat is okay)
Add and heat to 160 degrees:	2 (29 oz.) cans pumpkin 2 tbsp. sugar 2 tsp. salt 1 tsp. pepper 2 tsp. cinnamon
At 160 degrees, add:	Roux: 3 tbsp. flour mixed into 3 tbsp. melted butter
Reduce heat to 150 degrees:	1/2 pint Half & Half 1 cup slivered almonds

Garnish with toasted pumpkin seeds.
Serves 4-6

Turkey Rice Soup

Another great use for turkey leftovers, this soup also uses up all those vegetables in the fridge!

Cook in soup pot until fluffy, about 20 minutes:	1 cup water 1 cup chicken stock or broth 3/4 cup rice
Add to soup pot. Heat to slow boil, then turn down to a simmer for about 30 minutes:	1/4 cup red onion, chopped 1/2 red bell pepper, chopped 1/2 green bell pepper, chopped 1 tsp. garlic powder 1 tsp. thyme 1 tsp. sage 1/2 tsp. pepper 1 medium carrot, chopped 1 stalk celery, diced 1 lb. turkey, chopped 1 tsp. salt

Garnish with parsley
Serves 4-6.

Tomato Cheddar Soup

Smooth and creamy, tomato soups are always served on Fridays at the Colophon Cafe. This is a very easy recipe using canned soup with your additions. Saves time and tastes like it took hours.

Saute with butter in soup pot until tender:
- 1 medium onion, chopped
- 2 cloves garlic, chopped

Add to soup pot:
- 2 (10 oz.) cans tomato soup
- 1-1/2 cups water
- 1 (16 oz.) can diced tomatoes
- 1/4 cup chopped parsley
- 3/4 tsp. black pepper
- 1/4 tsp. thyme

Heat to boil, then add:
- 1/3 lb. cheddar, diced and tossed with flour
- 1/4 cup sherry

Serve immediately.

Garnish with a thin sliced cheddar cheese triangle.
Serves 4-6.

Cauliflower Cheddar Soup

An excellent cheese soup for cauliflower lovers.

In soup pot cook at a slow boil until potatoes are done, about 1/2 hour, in enough water to cover veggies:

- 1 potato, peeled & diced
- 2 cups cauliflower, cut small
- 1 carrot, peeled & chopped
- 2 cloves garlic, peeled & chopped
- 1/2 cup dried minced onion
- 1/4 cup instant potatoes
- 1/2 tsp. dill
- 1/2 tsp. pepper
- 1/2 tsp. salt

Reduce heat to 160 degrees. Stir into soup:

- Roux: 3 tbsp. flour mixed into 3 tbsp. melted butter

Thin with milk to desired consistency, and add 1/2 cup diced cheddar and a dash of Tabasco.

*Garnish with a cheddar wedge.
Serves 4-6.*

Tomato Rice Soup

Not like Mom used to make! This tomato soup utilizes an easy canned shortcut with additions of rice and herbs. Serve with crackers and it's lunch.

Cook in soup pot until fluffy, about 20 minutes:	2 cups water 3/4 cups pearl rice
Add to soup pot. Heat to slow boil then turn down to a simmer for about 30 minutes.	3 (10 3/4 oz.) cans tomato soup 1 (15 oz.) can diced tomatoes 1/2 cup minced onion 1/4 cup chopped parsley 1 tsp. garlic powder 1/2 tsp. black pepper 1 tsp. thyme

*Garnish with parsley.
Serves 4-6.*

Barbecue Ham Soup

An unusual use for barbecue sauce as a flavor enhancer in a soup. Serve as a main course with an exotic bread.

Cook in soup pot until fluffy, about 20 minutes:	4 cups chicken consommé 1 cup pearl rice
Soften on hot rice and whip smooth:	1/4 lb. cream cheese
Add and heat to 160 degrees:	2 cans water 1/2 cup minced onion 1/4 cup barbecue sauce 1/2 lb. ham, cut into 1/4 inch cubes
Add and heat to 150 degrees:	Roux: 3 tbsp. flour mixed into 3 tbsp. melted butter

Simmer for half an hour or longer, stirring gently once in a while.

Garnish with thin ham strips or a sprig of parsley
Serves 4-6.

Tomato Parmesan Soup

One more simple tomato soup utilizing canned short cuts and shredded Parmesan cheese. Fabulous eye appeal as a first course.

Add to soup pot. Heat to slow boil then turn down to a simmer for 30 minutes.

3 (15 oz.) cans tomato soup
2 cans water
15 oz. canned or fresh diced tomatoes

1 medium onion, minced
1/4 cup chopped parsley
2 cloves minced garlic
1/2 tsp. black pepper

Garnish with shredded Parmesan cheese or a sprig of parsley

Serves 4-6.

Substitutions

I didn't have potatoes,
So I substituted rice.
I didn't have paprika,
So I used another spice.
I didn't have tomato sauce,
So I used tomato paste.
A whole can, not a half can,
I don't believe in waste.
A friend gave me the recipe,
He said you couldn't beat it.
There must be something wrong
with him,
I couldn't even EAT it!

Vegetarian Soups

Christmas Corn Soup

This is a great winter soup for lunch or as a dinner first course, the yellow of the corn mixed with the red and green peppers make a visual delight as well as a hearty bowl of soup.

In a large pot, saute with olive oil until tender:	1/2 cup onion, chopped 1/4 cup each red & green peppers, chopped 2 cloves garlic, minced
Add and heat to 160 degrees:	1 (15 oz.) can creamed corn 1 can water 1/2 tsp. thyme 1/2 tsp. black pepper 1/2 tsp. tarragon
Add and heat to 150 degrees:	1 (20 oz.) pkg. frozen corn. Fresh or canned will also work, but will change the consistence of the soup.
Stir in:	Roux: 3 tbsp. flour mixed into 3 tbsp. melted butter

Simmer for half and hour or longer, stirring gently once in a while.

*Garnish with a sprig of fresh parsley.
Serves 4-6.*

Gazpacho

A spicy, cold tomato soup. Full of healthy veggies. Excellent for a summer meal.

Mix together the day before serving in a large bowl and chill overnight:

- 3 (15 oz.) cans diced tomatoes, or fresh tomatoes that have been peeled and chopped
- 46 oz. vegetable juice cocktail
- 1/4 cup white onion, chopped
- 3 cucumbers, peeled, seeded and diced
- 1/2 bunch celery, diced
- 1/4 bunch cilantro, minced
- 1 bunch green onions, chopped
- 2 tbsp. olive oil
- 2 tbsp. garlic, minced
- A good dash of Tabasco
- 1 tsp. salt
- 1 tsp. pepper

Hints: Thin with chilled vegetable juice if too thick. Chill pot and bowls in freezer before serving.
For variety try adding small shrimp or a dollop of sour cream on top.
Garnish with tortilla chips.

Serves 6-8

Italian Barley Soup

Grated carrots and diced tomatoes give this barley soup its own personality.

Cook covered in soup pot at a slow boil until tender, about 30 minutes:
- 3/4 cups barley
- 1/4 cup rice
- 4 cups water

Add and heat to 160 degrees:
- 1 (14-1/2 oz.) can diced tomatoes
- 2 (10-3/4 oz.) cans vegetable juice
- 3/4 cup grated carrots
- 2 cloves garlic, minced
- 2 tsp. oregano
- 1-1/2 tsp. basil
- 2 tbsp. parsley, chopped

Garnish with fresh parsley
Serves 4-6.

Mexican Corn & Bean Sopa

One of the most popular soups ever to come from the Colophon. The Mexican Corn & Bean Sopa has been featured in many publications since we created it. It's vegetarian and lowfat!

Sauté in a little olive oil in a large pot:	1 medium onion, finely diced 3 cloves garlic, minced
Add to pot and heat to a slow boil:	1 (15 oz.) can diced tomatoes or equal amount fresh tomatoes and juice 2 (15 oz.) cans red kidney beans, drained 1 (24 oz.) can vegetable juice
Mix together in a small bowl, then add hot water to a paste-like consistency, then add to pot:	3 tsp. chili powder 1 tsp. sugar 1/2 tsp. black pepper 1 tsp. cumin
Add to pot, heat to slow boil, reduce heat and simmer for about 20 minutes:	1 lb. bag frozen corn

Garnish with sour cream and tortilla chips.
Serves 4-6.

Colophon Croutons

The Colophon's own toasted garlic croutons are great on split pea soup as a garnish, or tossed in a caesar salad!

Cut enough bread into 3/4 inch cubes
and spread out on a cookie sheet,
1 layer thick.

Add : 3/4 cup melted butter
1 tbsp. garlic
1 tbsp. thyme
1 tbsp. parsley
1 tbsp. tarragon

Drizzle mixture over bread, stirring as you go.
Put in 400 degree oven for 8 minutes.
Stir well.
Put back in for 3 to 4 minutes
until they are golden toasty brown.
Leave out to cool.
Store in sealed containers.

Split Pea Soup

Split pea soup is so naturally good that the less you do to it the better.

Cook until peas are nearly done:
- 5 cups water
- 1 lb. green split peas, rinsed
- 1 medium onion, diced fine
- 1 tsp. salt
- 1 tsp. pepper

Add:
- 1 medium carrot, diced

Cook until carrots are done.

Thin with hot water if needed, but it should be as thick as fog!

Hey diddle diddle
I've a bulge in my middle
I hope to whittle it soon.
But eating's such fun,
I won't get it done,
'Til my dish runs away
   with my spoon!
      ... D. Neil

*Garnish with Colophon Croutons.
Serves 4-6.*

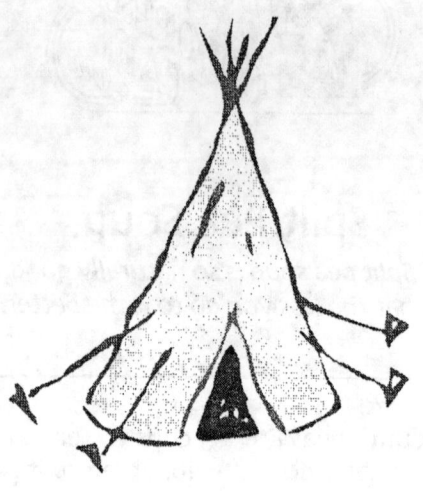

"A tepee is much better to live in: always clean, warm in winter, cool in summer; easy to move. Indians and animals know better how to live than white man; nobody can be in good health if he does not have all the time fresh air, sunshine, and good water."
 ... Flying Hawk

Mama Colophon

Three Sisters Soup

A Southwest Indian tradition featuring beans, corn & squash. They would plant them together in the same mound so they could support each other.

Combine and cook until beans are done:	1/4 lb. small red beans 1/4 lb. small white beans 3 cups water 1 medium yellow onion, chopped fine 3 cloves garlic, minced 1/3 tsp. nutmeg 1/4 tsp. paprika 1 tsp. salt 3/4 tsp. pepper
Add and heat to 160 degrees:	1 lb. bag frozen corn 29 oz. can pumpkin
Add and heat to 150 degrees:	Roux: 3 tbsp. flour mixed into 3 tbsp. melted butter
Finishing touch:	1/2 pint Half & Half

Garnish with toasted pumpkin seeds.
Serves 4-6

Green Onion Potato Dill Soup
Tangy with onions and dill, an inexpensive and hearty soup for a cold day.

In covered soup pot, cook potatoes until medium soft, in just enough water to cover:

4 potatoes, chopped

Add, bring to slow boil, reduce heat and simmer for 30 minutes:

1 bunch green onion, chopped
1/2 tsp. pepper
1/2 tsp. salt
1 tsp. tarragon
1 tsp. dill
1/4 cup instant potatoes

*Thin with water if needed.
Garnish with fresh dill.
Serves 4-6.*

Vegetarian Vegetable Soup

This soup is a vegetable lover's feast! Cook up a garden of nutritious and yummy soup. Make extra and freeze it for a later treat.

Cook in soup pot until potatoes are done:
- 1 cup potatoes, cut into 1/2 inch cubes
- 1/4 cup pearl barley
- 3 cups water
- 2 stalks celery, chopped
- 2 carrots, diced
- 2 cloves garlic, chopped
- 1 medium onion, chopped

Add, and heat to 160 degrees:
- 1 (15 oz.) can diced tomatoes
- 1 lb. fresh or frozen peas
- 1 tsp. black pepper
- 1/2 tsp. thyme
- 1/2 tsp. oregano
- 1/2 tsp. dill
- 1/2 tsp. marjoram

*Garnish with parsley.
Serves 4-6.*

Old Farmer's Saying:
A swarm of bees in May
  Is worth a load of hay;
A swarm of bees in June
  Is worth a silver spoon
A swarm of bees in July
  Is not worth a fly!

Tomato Florentine Soup

A twist on the unusual tomato soup everyone will appreciate. Herbs and spices perk it up and the pasta gives a hearty texture.

Cook at slow boil in a covered soup pot until spinach and onions are done.:
- 1 (1 lb.) pkg. frozen chopped spinach
- 1 can diced tomatoes
- 2 cans tomato soup
- 2 cans water
- 1 tsp. pepper
- 2 tsp. tarragon
- 1/2 tsp. basil
- 2 tsp. oregano
- 1/4 tsp. marjoram
- 2 tsp. garlic powder
- 1 medium yellow onion, diced fine
- Dash of Tabasco

Add pasta, simmer for 5-10 minutes before serving:
- 6 oz. cooked pasta shells (small or medium)

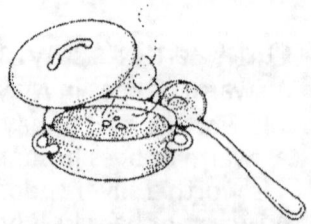

Garnish with grated Parmesan cheese.
Serves 4-6

Potato Leek Soup

*A delicious way to fix potatoes.
Use low fat chicken stock to cut calories and
serve with french bread.*

In covered soup pot, cook potatoes until medium soft, in just enough water and stock to cover:	4 diced potatoes 3 chopped leeks (discard dark green rough ends) 2 cups chicken stock 1/4 cup instant potatoes
Add, bring to slow boil, reduce heat and simmer 30 minutes:	1 tsp. tarragon 1 tsp. dill 1/2 tsp. pepper 1/2 tsp. salt 1/2 tsp. rosemary Dash Tabasco Roux: 1 tbsp. flour mixed into 1 tbsp. melted butter

Thin with milk.

*Garnish with parsley.
Serves 4-6*

"The time has come," the Walrus said, "to talk of many things: of shoes and ships and sealing wax, of cabbages and kings and why the sea is boiling hot, and whether pigs have wings."
. . . Lewis Carroll

Mama Colophon

Colophon Cabbage Soup

It's simple, it's healthy, it's cabbage.

In covered soup pot, cook potatoes until medium soft, in just enough water to cover:

4 cubed potatoes

Add, simmer 15 minutes:

1 small head cabbage, chopped
1 medium yellow onion, chopped
2 tsp. tarragon

Add, simmer 20-30 minutes, stirring occasionally:

1/2 bunch green onions, chopped
1/2 cup instant potatoes
Salt & pepper to taste

*Garnish with parsley
Serves 4-6.*

"Most definitely a two thumbs up kind of chili," he announced confidently, "and don't even think about putting any cow in it."

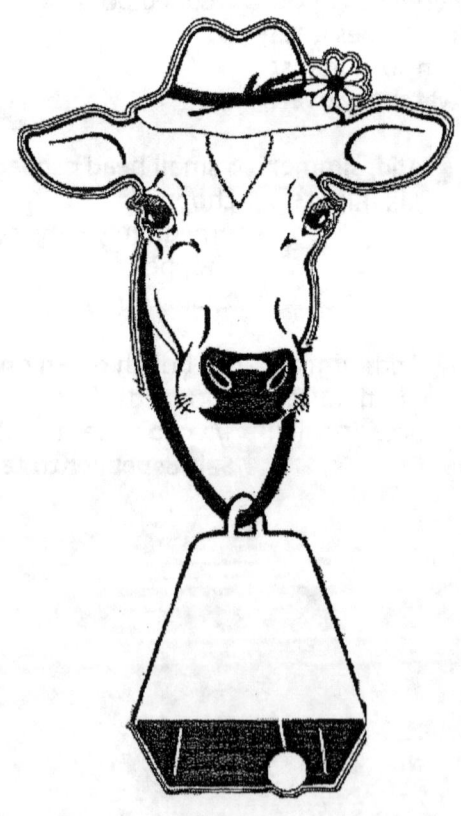

Exotic Soups

"Ancient drums echoed eerily through the lush green jungle as a scantily-clad Tarzan carefully stirred the thick soup in his tree-house kitchen, hoping fervently that Jane would swoon over his culinary efforts and melt into his arms in an uncontrollable passion."

From: *"Tarzan and the Magic Ginger Root,"* by Mama Colophon

Mama Colophon

The *Original* African Peanut Soup

This often-copied-never-duplicated recipe was created in the fall of 1985, to complement the movie playing across the street "Out of Africa." The ginger root, chilies and garlic give it a distinctive spicy taste which some people call "addictive." This recipe has appeared in other cookbooks, including the Colophon's Best Recipes.

Blend in food processor to create soup base:	1 oz. fresh ginger root, scrubbed and cut in chunks 2 cloves garlic 1 tsp. crushed chili peppers 3-1/4 cups canned or fresh diced tomatoes 1-3/4 cups dry roasted unsalted peanuts 1 small onion, chopped
Place soup base in pot. Add the following and cook to 165 degrees:	1-1/2 cups chicken stock 3 cups water
Make a Roux paste. Add to thicken:	Roux: 1/4 cup flour mixed into 1/4 cup melted butter
Finally, add:	2 cups diced tomatoes, canned or fresh 1/2 lb. cooked and cubed turkey or chicken

Hint: Whisk warm Roux into soup and simmer to thicken.
Add final tomatoes to thin and to add chunkiness to soup.
Thin with water to desired consistency.
For vegetarian version, leave out the turkey or chicken, and use vegetable stock instead of chicken stock.
Garnish with peanuts.
Serves 6-8

Spicy Thai Rice Soup

A wonderful peanut rice soup flavored with spicy ginger root, onions and peppers.

Combine in soup pot and cook for 20 minutes:
- 1-1/4 cups rice
- 3 cups water

Chop in food processor, then add to soup pot:
- 2 carrots
- 2 oz. ginger root
- 1 medium onion
- 1 bell pepper
- 3 cloves garlic
- 1 tsp. cumin
- 2 tsp. curry
- 1 tsp. black pepper
- 1 tsp. salt
- Dash of cayenne pepper
- 1/4 lb. peanut butter

Heat to a slow boil. Thin with 2 cups water, and simmer for 30 minutes or longer.

*Garnish with peanuts.
Serves 4-6.*

Colophon Curried Carrot

Our more popular carrot soup. This has become a favorite among vegetarians and carnivores alike.

Cook rice until done. Approx. 20 minutes.	1/3 cup parboiled white rice 2/3 cup water
In separate pot, cook vegetables until tender	2 large carrots, diced 1/2 red pepper, diced 1/2 green pepper, diced 1 tsp. ginger root, minced 1/4 cup sun-dried tomatoes, diced

After rice and vegetables are cooked, combine and puree in a food processor. Then return to soup pot.

Combine vegetables with rice, then add. Cook to 165°.	8 oz. vegetable stock 2/3 tsp. green curry paste 1 tsp. curry powder 2/3 tsp granulated garlic 2/3 tsp. salt Pinch of thyme 3/4 cup coconut milk

For garnish, thin some sour cream by whisking in some half & half or milk, then drizzle over the top of soup. Add a fresh sprig of parsley.
Serves 4-6.

Mediterranean Vegetable Soup

Take a trip to Italy with this exotic soup.

Cook until rice is done:	1/2 cup rice 1 cup water 1 cup vegetable stock
Bring to a slow boil, reduce heat and simmer for 30 minutes:	1/4 cup sundried tomatoes 1 stalk celery, chopped 1 green pepper, chopped 3 cucumbers, peeled, diced, seeded and processed in food processor or finely chopped 1/4 cup feta cheese, chopped fine 3 tsp. garlic powder 1/2 tsp. pepper 2 tsp. salt Juice from 1/2 lemon 1 tsp. oregano

Garnish with thin cucumber slices.
Serves 4-6.

Jamaican Red Bean Soup

Red beans and ham flavor this island inspired dish. Serve it with a good beer and some tortilla chips, with papaya salsa on the side!

Cook in soup pot 30-40 minutes until beans are done:	1 lb. red beans 5 cups water
Add, then bring to a slow boil, reduce heat and simmer for 45 minutes to an hour:	1 onion, chopped 2 red bell peppers, diced 3 cloves garlic, minced 1/4 lb. diced ham 1 stalk celery, chopped 1/8 cup parsley, chopped 1 tsp. thyme 1/2 tsp. salt 1 tsp. pepper Dash of Tabasco

Thin with hot water as soup reduces.

Garnish with parsley.
Serves 4-6.

Curried Turkey & Apple Soup

A Colophon favorite for many years, this dairy-free soup has an unusual apple and curry flavor, invented by our chef after enjoying some curried turkey apple crepes.

Cook in soup pot until fluffy, about 20 minutes:
- 2 cups water
- 3/4 cups pearl rice
- 1-1/2 cups chicken stock or consommé

Add, and bring to a slow boil, reduce heat and simmer for 30 minutes:
- 1 small red onion, minced
- 1 medium carrot, peeled and chopped
- 1 tsp. salt
- 2 tsp. cinnamon
- 1 tsp. black pepper
- 2 tsp. thyme
- 1/4 tsp. Tabasco sauce
- 3 tbsp. curry
- 2 granny smith apples, cored, peeled & chopped
- 1 lb. turkey, cooked & cubed

Thin with water as needed.

Garnish with dry chow mein noodles.
Serves 4-6.

Avgolemono

(ahv-go LEH-mo-no)
No matter how you pronounce it, this classic Greek egg and lemon soup, made with rice and chicken, is said to cure the worst cold!

Cook about 20 minutes until rice is fluffy:
- 1/2 cup rice
- 2 cups chicken stock
- 1 cup water

Add and heat to a slow boil, reduce heat and simmer for 20 minutes:
- 1/2 lb. chopped cooked chicken

Combine and add 1 cup of the hot chicken stock to eggs, then stir all back into soup mixture:
- 2 whole raw eggs
- 1/4 cup lemon juice

Garnish with parsley.
Serves 4-6.

Curried Banana Soup

Okay, it's odd, it's exotic, and you can impress your dinner guests with it.

Sauté in butter until tender in large soup pot:	3 cloves garlic, minced 1 medium onion, minced
Cook until fluffy, about 20 minutes:	1-1/2 cups water 3/4 cup pearl rice
Add, and heat to a slow boil, reduce heat and simmer for 30 minutes:	3 cups water 2 tsp. lemon juice 1 tsp. salt 3 1/2 tsp. curry 1/2 tbsp. pepper 3 ripe bananas, chopped fine 2 tsp. dried basil Dash of cinnamon
Add, then whip:	Roux: 4 tbsp. flour mixed into 3 tbsp. melted butter
Add, then heat to 150 degrees: DO NOT BOIL	1 pint Half & Half

Garnish with dried banana chips.
Serves 4-6.

Thai Ginger Chicken Soup

This extraordinary, exotic soup won the 1995 Allied Arts Soup Festival in Bellingham.

Cook until rice is done:	2-1/2 cups chicken broth 1 cup rice
Add to soup pot cook, until temperature reaches 160 degrees:	1 tbsp. "Taste of Thai" Green Curry Base[+] 1 tbsp. garlic powder 2 tsp. thyme 2 tsp. basil 1 tbsp. fresh ground ginger root 1 lb. chopped cooked chicken
Turn heat down slightly and add:	1 (14 oz.) can coconut milk Dash of lime juice Dash of lemon juice

Serve at 150 degrees. Thin with water if desired. Rice will make mixture very thick.

[+] *Curry base contains: chilies. onion, garlic galanga, lemon kaffir, and lime peel. We sell it at the Colophon if you can't find it.*

Garnish with fresh parsley.
Serves 4-6.

Best Recipes
Alphabetical Index

African Peanut, The Original 61
Almond, Cream of 20
Asparagus Bisque 22
Avgolemono 67
Banana, Curried 68
Barbecue Ham 40
Beer Cheese (Cheddar Ale) 31
Black Bean Chili 16
Broccoli, Cream of 21
Butter Bean Dijon 33
Cabbage, Colophon 57
Carrot, Colophon 63
Cauliflower Cheddar 38
Chicken Mushroom, Cream of . . 26
Christmas Corn 44
Clam Chowder 8
Corn Chili 11
Corn Chowder, Vegan 9
Croutons, Colophon 48
Curried Corn and Cheddar 10
Dill Pickle, Cream of 23
Gazpacho 45
Green Onion Potato Dill 52
Italian Barley 46

Jamaican Red Bean 65
Kielbasa Bean 34
Lemon Chicken Rice 32
Lentil Chili 15
Manhattan Clam Chowder . . . 11
Mediterranean Vegetable 64
Mexican Corn and Bean 47
Mushroom, Cream of 25
Potato Leek 55
Pumpkin Almond 35
Spicy Thai Rice 62
Spinach, Cream of 27
Split Pea 49
Thai Ginger Chicken 69
Three Sisters 51
Tomato Cheddar 37
Tomato Florentine 54
Tomato Rice 39
Tomato Parmesan 41
Turkey Almondine 24
Turkey Apple, Curried 66
Turkey Chili, Ray's 17
Turkey Rice 36
Vegetarian Vegetable 53

A big thank you to all Colophon staff, past and present, who contributed their culinary knowledge and special recipes to the Colophon Cafe. Thanks also to our many customers around the world, whose thoughtful comments and appreciative palates made this book possible.

MAMA COLOPHON
(our founder)

Notes

The Colophon Cafe
Best Vegetarian Recipes

by

Ray Dunn & Taimi Dunn Gorman

COLOPHON: (kol 'e fon')
1. A publisher's distinctive emblem.
2. An inscription at the end of a book, usually with facts relative to its publication.
3. Greek koloph'on: summit, finishing touch, the last word.
   (pronounced "Call- a-fawn" Cafe)

MAMA COLOPHON
(our founder)

1208 11th Street (Fairhaven)
Bellingham, Washington 98225
360-647-0092

For more recipes and information, log on to ColophonCafe.com

First published by Mama Colophon, Inc. 1998.
All rights reserved.
This facsimile edition published by Chuckanut Editions, 2012.

These recipes may be reproduced for personal use only.

*A big thank you to all Colophon staff, past and present, who contributed their culinary knowledge and special recipes to the Colophon Cafe.
Thanks also to our many customers around the world, whose thoughtful comments and appreciative palates made this book possible!*

MAMA COLOPHON
(our founder)

"Nowhere can I think so happily as in a train...I see a cow, and I wonder what it is like to be a cow, and I wonder whether the cow wonders what it is like to be me."

-A.A. Milne

Best Vegetarian Recipes
of The Colophon Cafe

Introduction

When we set out to do a vegetarian cookbook, we had do to some research. There are many types of vegetarians. Some do not eat any animal products, and others include dairy or seafood into their diets. The Colophon Cafe developed part of its fame by offering vegetarian dishes that would suit almost everyone.

After some discussion, we decided that some recipes using dairy products would be accepted for this book. We hope we've chosen foods most people will be happy to fix for their families and friends, and we've tried to make them as easy as possible to prepare and still maintain their excellence.

The new Vegetarian Diet Pyramid recommends including whole fruits, vegetables, grains and legumes at each meal. Nuts, seeds, egg whites, soy milk, dairy products and plant oils are recommended daily. Egg yolks and sweets may be included occasionally. We've tried to include most of these healthy foods in our dishes to help you plan meals.

The recipes were collected from items we serve already, favorites of our staff and friends and generally anything we love to cook. Ray Dunn's influence is big in this book because of his travels to exotic locales and the cooking he's experienced all over the world.

We hope you will enjoy this book! Happy dining!

"Paradise is where I am."
Voltaire, 1694-1774

Best Vegetarian Recipes

Contents

Alphabetical Index on page 80

Appetizers
Galloping Guacamole..................................2
Spicy Quesadillas......................................3
Jumping Jalapenos....................................5
Chili Relleno Cheese Bars.........................6
Pigeon Peas Accra....................................7
Baked Almond Brie...................................9
Cheese Straws...10
Corn Fritters..11
Chili Cheese Dip......................................13

Soups
Split Pea Soup...17
Colophon Croutons.................................17
Gazpacho...18
Mexican Corn & Bean Sopa....................19
Spicy Thai Rice Soup..............................21
Almond Bean Soup.................................23
Syrian Lentil Soup..................................25

Salads
Turkish Cucumber Salad.........................28
Finnish Wilted Cucumber Salad.............29
Orange & Radish Salad...........................31
Green Bean & Tomato Salad...................32
Avocado Caesar Salad.............................35
Potato Cheese Salad................................36
Chilled Vegetable Pasta Salad.................37

Side Dishes
Spicy Peanut Sauce..40
Vegetarian Potstickers......................................41
Hawaiian Rice...42
Cinnamon Rice...43
Hummus..44
Spinach in Sour Cream....................................45
Spicy Oven Fries...46
Coconut Milk Garlic Mashed Potatoes...........47
Pumpkin Blueberry Corn Bread......................49
Honey Rum Butter..49
Oregon Zucchini Cashew Bread.....................51
Herbed Tomato Barbecue Sauce....................52
Barbecued Vegetable Skewers........................53

Entrees
Quick Broccoli Cheddar Quiche....................57
Broccoli Cheddar Pot Pie...............................58
Pot Pie Parmesan Biscuit Topping..................59
Chili Relleno...60
Sweet Onion Enchiladas.................................61
Jamaican Red Beans & Rice..........................62
Spanakopita..63
Black Bean Taquitos con Guacamole............64
Chunky Guacamole..65
Asian Noodle Salad..66
Mushroom Casserole......................................67

Desserts
Finnish Apple Pie..71
Peach Oat Crisp..72
Pumpkin Pone...73
Dave's Breakfast Cookies...............................74
Bapple Cookies...75
Colophon Peanut Butter Pie...........................76
Chocolate Cookie Crust..................................77
Peanut Butter Chocolate Brownies.................78
Mom's Jamocha Rum Cake...........................79

Appetizers

"*He who comes first, eats first.*"
Eike von Repkow, 1219-1233,
Sachsenspiegel

Galloping Guacamole

Numerous trips to Mexico have only increased our fondness for this traditional dish.

Take the outer peel off the avocados, remove pits. Mash them with the back of a fork.

Remove the seed from the chilies before you chop them unless you want a full gallop.

Stir in chilies, onion, lime juice, cumin, chili powder and salt.

If you are not serving the guacamole right away cover it tightly with clear wrap, pushing the wrap lightly onto the mixture to keep it from turning dark.

Use the green leafy stuff to line a platter or bowl with the guacamole in the center.

2 large avocados
  or 4 small ones

1/2 red onion, diced
1 teaspoon cumin
1 teaspoon chili powder
1 or 2 finely chopped
  canned whole green
  chilies
2 Tablespoons lime juice
1 teaspoon salt

some green leafy stuff like
  lettuce

Serve with tortilla chips and a good Mexican Beer.

Serves 4

Spicy Quesadillas

*Quesadilla quarters make yummy appetizers, especially with guacamole and salsa.
The spicy Jack cheese and chili powder give these a bite.*

Pour one tablespoon oil in the bottom of a sauce pan and heat to medium. Cook onion in oil until soft. Stir in cumin, chili powder and refried beans until mixture is hot.

Heat 2 tablespoons olive oil in skillet. Add one tortilla and cook 30 seconds. Turn over. Evenly spread half the bean mixture from sauce pan and half the cheese onto one tortilla. Top with second tortilla and flip over on pan. Cook until brown. Repeat with remaining tortillas.

Cut into quarters for serving.

Top with dab of guacamole.

3 Tablespoons olive oil
1 medium onion, chopped
3/4 teaspoon cumin
1 teaspoon chili powder
1 cup vegetarian refried beans

4 flour tortillas

1 1/2 cups hot pepper Jack cheese, grated

**Makes 8 quarter pieces
Serves four as an appetizer**

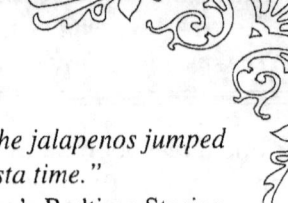

"In old Mexico, even the jalapenos jumped for joy when it was fiesta time."
　　　Mama Colophon's Bedtime Stories

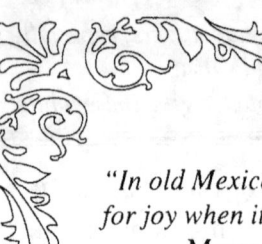

MAMA COLOPHON
(our founder)

Jumping Jalapenos

Party food of the most colorful kind.

---

12 large, fresh jalapenos
1/2 cup nonfat cream cheese, softened
1/4 cup shredded mozzarella
1/4 cup grated parmesan cheese
vegetable cooking spray
salsa

Cut peppers in half lengthwise; remove seeds. Combine cheeses, spoon evenly into pepper halves.

Place halves in a 13"x 9" x 2" inch baking dish coated with cooking spray. Bake uncovered at 350° for 30 minutes or until bubbly and lightly browned.

Serve warm with salsa and beer.

Makes twenty four

Chili Relleno Cheese Bars

Another fast recipe that makes the house smell great as it cooks.

Preheat oven to 400 degrees. Spray 8 inch square pan with vegetable oil spray. Beat the eggs in a mixing bowl until smooth. Gradually add cottage cheese, flour and baking powder. Beat until smooth.

Stir in chilies and the next three ingredients. Pour into pan. Bake uncovered at 400° for 15 minutes; reduce heat to 350° and bake for 35 more minutes or until firm. Let stand 15 minutes. Cut into 12 bars. Serve warm with salsa.

4 eggs
1 cup cottage cheese
1/4 cup flour
1/ teaspoon baking powder

1 4.5 oz can chopped green chilies, drained
1/2 teaspoon hot sauce
1/3 cup shredded mozzarella
1/3 cup shredded sharp cheddar

salsa

Serves 6

Pigeon Peas Accra

A favorite appetizer from the Island of Tobago

Crush peas with fork, add all other ingredients, mix well.

Fry by spoonfuls in hot oil.

Garnish with almost any thing: parsley, chopped hard boiled eggs, sliced black olives, crushed nuts.

Serve hot.

1 cup pigeon peas
  or 1 cup green peas
1 medium onion, chopped
2 eggs, beaten
1 stalk celery, chopped
1/2 cup flour
1 teaspoon baking powder
1/2 teaspoon salt
1/4 cup liquid from peas

Serves 4

"Cows are my passion."
Dombey and Son
Charles Dickens, 1848

Baked Almond Brie

Purely decadent, creamy and crunchy simultaneously, this brie deserves to accompany a really good champagne.

Broil almonds in toaster oven or regular oven on baking sheet only until brown and fragrant. Watch carefully so they don't burn.

Heat regular oven to 350″
Place brie on round plate and slice off white crust on top.

Sprinkle toasted almonds liberally on top of cheese.

Turn off oven. Place brie in warm oven and let gently melt until soft but not runny, about 10 minutes.

Put hot plate onto larger plate and surround with sliced apples, pears or crackers.

1- 2 ounce package slivered almonds

1- 15 ounce round brie cheese

Sliced apples, pears or crackers

Serves 10 or more as an appetizer.

Cheese Straws

A very simple yet delicious appetizer, this is a good one to make with young help on a rainy day.
Recipe may be doubled.

Rub butter into flour, add cheese and seasoning. Bind to a stiff paste with the egg yolk and water, Roll out thinly and cut into straws.
Bake in a 375° oven for about 5 to 7 minutes.

Serve hot.

4 Tablespoons flour
4 Tablespoons butter
4 Tablespoons grated cheese
  (any kind will do but hard cheeses seem to work best)
about 1/2 an egg yolk.
salt & pepper
a little water

Makes appetizers for about four.

Corn Fritters

Serve as a prelude to a Southern style dinner or as a side dish with a bean chili.

Sift flour, baking powder and salt together.
Beat eggs until fluffy.
Add beaten eggs, pepper and melted butter to dry ingredients and beat with a fork until smooth.
Stir in creamed corn. (Batter should be of a dropping consistency. Add a bit of milk if it needs thinning.)
Drop by spoonfuls into preheated oil (375°) in a large frying pan

Fry for 4 or 5 minutes or until evenly browned. Serve hot by themselves or with a dip of your choosing.

1 1/2 cups flour
2 teaspoons baking powder
1/2 teaspoons salt
1/4 teaspoons pepper
2 eggs
1 Tablespoon melted butter
1 -1/2 cups creamed corn

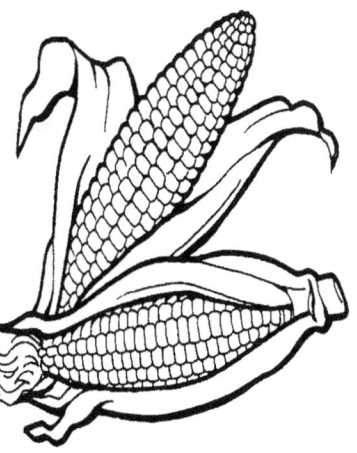

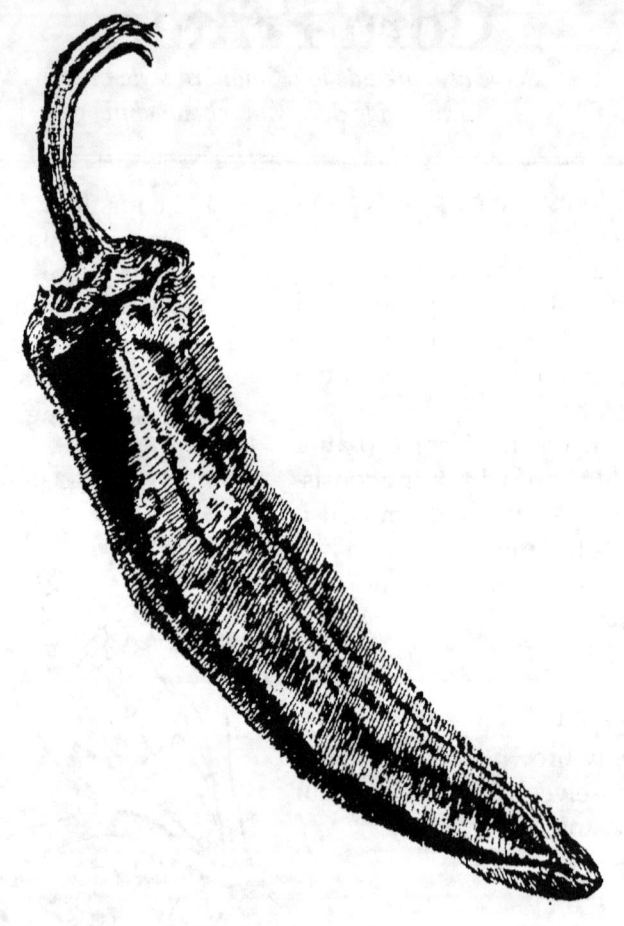

Chili Cheese Dip

You can make this ahead and refrigerate overnight for a "pop-it-in-the-oven easy" appetizer.

On the bottom of a 9" x 13" pan spread the cream cheese. Layer the chili on top of it; Place the diced green chiles on top of the chili. Top with the grated cheddar.

May be refrigerated for later use.

Before serving, place in a 350° oven and bake for 30 minutes. During the last 5 minutes of baking, add garnishes and return to oven. Serve it right away with a basket of tortilla chips and a cold Mexican beer. For more than 6 people you might want to make 2, because the first one will go faster than Poncho Villa at a taco-eating contest.

2 - 16 ounce packages of cream cheese, softened
2 - 12 ounce cans vegetarian chili, or make your own.
1 small can diced green chilies
2 cups grated cheddar

Sliced black olives and green onions for garnish

Tortilla chips

Soup is the path to everyone's heart.

"Oliver Twist has asked for more!"
Charles Dickens, 1837

Split Pea Soup
Thick as Fog!

Our simple, healthy version created by Ray Dunn is vegetarian and low-fat. We garnish it with our own homemade croutons.

Lightly saute in a little butter	1 cup finely diced yellow onion
Bring to a boil. Cook covered on simmer for 1 to 1 1/2 hours or until carrots are done.	5 cups water 1 pound green split peas (rinsed) 1 medium carrot, diced salt & pepper to taste
Thin with water	

Serves 6-8
Garnish with Colophon Croutons.

Colophon Croutons
Use as a garnish for soups or salads.

Cube enough day-old bread to cover a cookie sheet.
Put the bread cubes in a large bowl.
Mix together:
1/2 cup melted butter
1 teaspoon each of garlic, thyme, parsley and tarragon

Drizzle butter mixture over bread, stiring cubes around.
Spread evenly onto cookie sheet.
Bake at 400° for 8 minutes. Stir well. Put back in oven until toasty brown. Cool before serving.

Gazpacho

A spicy, cold tomato soup full of healthy veggies. Excellent for a summer meal.

Mix together in a large bowl the day before serving and chill overnight.

- 3 -15 ounce cans diced tomatoes or fresh tomatoes that have been peeled and chopped
- 46 ounce vegetable juice cocktail
- 1/4 cup chopped white onion
- 3 cucumbers, peeled, seeded, diced
- 1/2 bunch celery, diced
- 1/4 bunch cilantro, minced
- 1 bunch green onions, chopped
- 2 Tablespoons olive oil
- 2 Tablespoons minced garlic
- A good dash Tabasco
- 1 teaspoon salt
- 1 teaspoon pepper

Thin with chilled vegetable juice if too thick. Chill pot and bowls in freezer before serving. For variety add a dollop of sour cream on top.

Garnish with Tortilla Chips

Serves 8-10

Mexican Corn and Bean Sopa

One of the most popular soups ever to come from the Colophon, the Mexican Corn & Bean Sopa has been featured in many publications since we created it. It's low in fat and delicious. We've made it fast to prepare, too.

Saute in a little olive oil	1 medium finely diced onion 3 cloves minced garlic
Add to soup pot and heat to a slow boil	1-15 ounce can diced tomatoes (or equal amount of chopped fresh tomatoes and tomato juice. 2- 15 ounce can red kidney beans (drained) 1- 24 ounce can vegetable juice
Mix spices in a small bowl, then add hot water to a paste-like consistency, Add to pot and heat	3 teaspoons chili powder 1 teaspoon sugar 1 teaspoon cumin 1/2 teaspoon black pepper
Add to pot; heat to 160° Simmer for 1 to 2 hours.	1 lb bag of frozen corn kernals

Thin with water or vegetable juice

**Garnish with blue and yellow Tortilla Chips
Serves 6-8**

"And it never mattered how cold it was, or how much it snowed, because Mama Bear always had something hot on the stove to keep them warm."
   Mama Colophon's Bedtime Stories

MAMA COLOPHON
(our founder)

Spicy Thai Rice Soup

A wonderful peanut rice soup flavored with spicy ginger root, onions and peppers.

Combine in soup pot cook 20 minutes	1-1/4 cups rice 3 cups water
Chop remaining ingredients in food processor then add to soup pot.	2 carrots 2 ounces ginger root 1 medium onion 1 bell pepper 3 cloves garlic 1 teaspoon cumin 2 teaspoon curry 1 teaspoon black pepper
Heat to a slow boil thin with 2 cups water, and simmer for 30 minutes or longer	1 teaspoon salt a dash of cayenne pepper 4 ounces peanut butter

Garnish with peanuts

Serves 4-6

"The natives took a big black pot they'd gotten from a whaling vessel, had the suprised missionaries for dinner, and decided shortly after that eating vegetarian tasted a whole lot better."
　　Mama Colophon's Bedtime Stories

Almond Bean Soup

Cover the beans in water and soak over night.

Drain the beans and cook them in the vegetable broth until tender.

Crush almonds in a blender or pound them to pieces. Stir the almonds into the beans.

Add the leeks, garlic, sugar and wine. Cook 10 more minutes, then put through a strainer or serve as is.

Garnish with 1 tablespoon of sour cream in each bowl.

1/2 cup navy beans

3 cups vegetable broth

3/4 cups blanched almonds

2 large leeks, finely chopped
1 garlic clove, minced
1 teaspoon sugar
1/2 cup white wine
1/2 cup sour cream
salt and pepper to taste

Serves 4

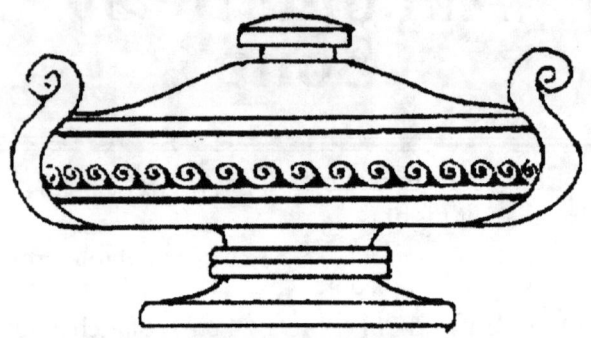

"In Damascus, Popeye won the best soup award with by adding spinach to lentils."
Mama Colophon's Bedtime Stories

MAMA COLOPHON
(our founder)

Syrian Lentil Soup

Wash and clean the lentils. Cover with cold water and cook slowly uncovered until tender.

Wash spinach leaves and break them up into small pieces. Add these and 1 cup of water to the lentils. Continue cooking until the spinach is done, adding more water if necessary.

Heat the olive oil in a skillet and add the onion, garlic, celery and salt, cook until tender and blended. Add this to the lentils. Mix the lemon juice with the flour stir it into the soup.

Cook gently stirring occasionally until the soup is rather thick.

Garnish with a sprinkle of parmesan cheese.

1 1/2 cups dried lentils
2 1/2 pounds spinach
1/4 cup olive oil
3/4 cup onion (chopped)
4 cloves garlic (chopped)
1 stalk celery (chopped)
3/4 cup lemon juice
1 -teaspoon flour
chopped chives

Serves 6

Salads

"My salad days, when I was green in judgement."
Shakespeare, Antony & Cleopatra I v 73

Turkish Cucumber Salad

Take a trip to Turkey with this great salad

Peel, split and scoop out the seeds of the cukes. Cut in very thin slices or long shreds. Put in a colander, sprinkle with the salt, and let drain for 1 or 2 hours. Then rinse briefly under cold water, drain again and pat dry.

Mix the yogurt with the pepper and lemon juice. Combine with the cucumbers, mint and parsley. Marinate several hours before serving

2 large cucumbers
2 teaspoons salt

1 cup yogurt
1/4 teaspoon freshly ground black pepper
1 Tablespoon lemon juice
1 Tablespoon fresh mint
1 Tablespoon chopped parsley

MAMA COLOPHON
(our founder)

Serves 4

Finnish Wilted Cucumber Salad

Wilted cucumbers are quite yummy.

Peel, split and scoop out the seeds of the cukes. Cut in very thin slices or long shreds. Put in a colander, sprinkle with the salt, and let drain for 1 or 2 hours. Then rinse briefly under cold water, drain again and pat dry.

Make a sweet and sour dressing with the rest of the ingredients. Pour the dressing over the cucumbers, cover with plastic wrap, and let stand for at least 3 hours before serving, by which time the cukes will have wilted.

2 large cucumbers
2 teaspoons salt

1/2 cup cider vinegar
2 Tablespoons water
3 Tablespoons sugar
1/4 teaspoon freshly ground black pepper
2 Tablespoons chopped dill
2 Tablespoons chopped parsley

Serves 4

Famous Cucumber Quotes:
"As cold as cucumbers."
Beaumont & Fletcher, 1615
Cupid's Revenge -act I

"But not near as tasty."
Mama Colophon's Bedtime Stories.

"Tis the time of salads."
Laurence Stern
Tristram Shandy, book 1

Orange & Radish Salad

Put lemon juice in a bowl and stir in the sugar and salt until completly dissolved.

1/3 cup lemon juice
2 Tablespoons sugar
1/4 teaspoon sugar

Using a sharp knife, cut off the peel and pithy part of the oranges, and slice them into bite size sections. Wash the radishes, trim off the tops and grate coarsely.

4 large navel oranges
1 bunch red radishes

Combine the oranges and radishes in a salad bowl, pour the lemon mixture over them and mix gently. Refrigerate until chilled. Serve very cold.

Serves 4

Green Bean & Tomato Salad

Prepare the dressing 2 or more hours before serving. Put all ingredients, except the oil, in a jar or cruet with lid, and shake to dissolve the salt, sugar and mustard. Add the oil and shake again.

Trim the beans and cut into 1-inch pieces. Drop them into a pot of rapidly boiling salted water. Boil uncovered, until just tender to the bite, about 5 to 7 minutes from the time the water returns to a rolling boil. Drain and run cold water over the beans, then dry thoroughly.

Remove the garlic and shake dressing just before adding. Toss with the salad. Cover and refrigerate 3 to 4 hours.

Dressing:
2 cloves garlic peeled and cut in half
1/2 teaspoon sugar
1/8 teaspoon dry mustard
1/8 teaspoon oregano
1 Tablespoon grated onion
1 Tablespoon lemon juice
2 Tablespoon red wine vinegar
1/4 cup olive oil

Salad:
1 pound green beans
3 Tablespoons green onion finely chopped
2 Tablespoons Blue cheese crumbled
3 ripe tomatoes sliced thin
Lettuce leaves

Green Bean & Tomato Salad (continued)

To Serve:
Line salad plates with lettuce leaves.
Top with a ring of overlapping tomato slices. Spoon a mound of the bean salad onto the center of the tomato slices.

Garnish with the egg slices, pimientos and olives.

Garnish:
2 hard boiled eggs, sliced
2 ounce jar sliced pimientos, drained

12 ripe black olives

Serves 4

"I came, I saw, I conquered."
Julius Caesar, 100-44 B.C.

MAMA COLOPHON
(our founder)

"I came, I saw, I ate"
Mama Colophon's Bedtime Stories

The Best Avocado Caesar Salad

No eggs needed in this one. We like it with heavy garlic, so use less if you don't want to taste it all day. Also, many people put the dressing in the bowl first and then add the lettuce. That's fine if you want most of the dressing to stay in the bowl. We prefer to drizzle over the top, then toss.

Prep lettuce into big bowl.

Salad:
2 large heads of green leaf or romaine lettuce, washed throughly, dried and torn into bite size bits.

Mix dressing ingredients together in cruet with lid and shake until blended. May be done hours ahead and held in refrigerator.

Dressing:
1/3 cup olive oil
6 garlic cloves, pressed or minced
3 teaspoons lemon juice
1 teaspoon Worcestershire sauce
Freshly ground pepper to taste

1 cup shredded parmesan cheese

Drizzle dressing over lettuce in bowl. Toss together with parmesan. Garnish top of salad with avocado slices and croutons if you wish.

2 or 3 peeled, sliced ripe avocados
Croutons

Serve with French bread.

Serves 6

Potato Cheese Salad

This tasty salad is great in the summertime, Chill well in advance and take it out for a picnic or a sunset cruise

Peel dice and boil potatoes until nearly fork tender.

Drain water and mix in cheese gently.

Cut up egg and add with other ingredients to the potato mixture.

Chill well before serving

4 medium potatoes
2 Tablespoons mayonnaise
2 Tablespoons yellow mustard
2 Tablespoon green pepper
2 Tablespoons red pepper
   (both finely chopped)
3 green onions, chopped
1/2 cup grated cheddar
1 hard boiled egg

Serves 6

Chilled Vegetable Pasta Salad

A cold pasta salad to make the day before.

Cook spaghetti and drain.

6 ounces spaghetti noodles

Combine oil, vinegar and spices in cruet with lid and shake. Pour over warm spaghetti. Cool in refrigerator.

1/3 cup vegetable oil
1/4 cup cider vinegar
1/2 teaspoon basil
1/4 teaspoon black pepper

3/4 cup chopped tomato
1/2 cup chopped celery
1/2 cup chopped cucumber
1/3 cup chopped green onion
1/4 cup chopped fresh parsley

Toss vegetables in cool spaghetti and chill throughly before serving.

Garnish with tomato wedges and parmesan to taste.

tomato wedges

parmesan cheese

Serves 6

Serves 6 as a main course

Spicy Peanut Sauce

Though traditionally used for Chicken Satay, our favorite Thai sauce can accompany raw vegetables or the vegetable potstickers on the next page.

Gently melt peanut butter in bottom of saucepan.

Add all other ingredients.

Heat on medium-high until thick, stirring often.

1/2 cup smooth peanut butter

1/2 Tablespoon chili powder
3 garlic cloves, pressed or chopped
1 1/4 cup coconut milk
1/4 cup soy sauce
1 Tablespoon lime juice

Makes about two cups of sauce.

Vegetarian Potstickers

These may be filled with nearly anything from the garden.

Heat 2 Tablespoons oil in saute pan at medium heat.

Stir fry all vegetables until softened.

In a bowl, combine garlic and vinegar with cooked vegetables.

Lay wonton wrappers on towel and place small amounts of vegetables in center of each. Wet edges of wrappers with water and crimp seams together tightly.

Reheat saute pan at medium. Coat pan with olive oil. Cook potstickers until browned. Add water and soy sauce and cover. Steam about 2 minutes. Remove and drain excess moisture off.

Potstickers are slippery. Serve them on separate plates for each guest. Chopsticks are good implements for those who can use them.

2 Tablespoons olive oil

1 medium zucchini diced
1 red bell pepper diced
1 med red onion peeled and diced
3 medium carrots diced

2 cloves minced garlic
2 Tablespoons balsamic vinegar

1 package won ton wrappers
small bowl water

1 cup water
1/4 cup soy sauce
1/4 cup olive oil

**Serves 8-10 as a side dish or appetizer.
Great served dipped in peanut sauce.**

Hawaiian Rice

Take a trip to the islands!
May be served with vegetables stir fried in terriaki sauce

Prepare rice according to package instructions, adding pineapple juice in place of part of the water.

When rice is cooked and water absorbed, stir in pineapple chunks.

Pour rice onto platter and garnish with macadamia nuts.

1 cup Jasmati rice
1 cup water
1 cup pineapple juice
1 Tablespoon butter
dash salt

1 cup pineapple chunks
1 cup macadamia nuts

Makes about 5 cups of rice.

Cinnamon Rice

Sinfully delicious.

Melt two tablespoons butter in deep sauce pan over medium heat.

4 Tablespoons butter

Reduce heat, add carrots, celery and onion and cook covered for 10 minutes. Stir occasionally.

1/2 cup diced carrots
1/2 cup diced celery
1/2 cup diced white onion

Add rice, salt, cinnamon, and water to pan and bring to a boil over high heat. When the water has reduced to the level of the rice, lower heat, cover and cook 15 to 20 minutes, stirring occasionally. Just prior to serving, add remaining butter.

2 cups long grain rice
1/2 teaspoon salt
1 Tablespoon ground cinnamon
1/2 cup golden raisins
6 cups water

Makes about 8 cups of rice.

Hummus

An exotic blend of healthy stuff that tastes great on bagels, as a vegetable dip, or on cucumber sandwiches.

Puree in food processor for 3 to 4 minutes.	4 cups cooked, drained garbonzo beans 2 teaspoons cumin 2 teaspoons salt 1/2 cup minced garlic 1 cup olive oil
Add	1-15 oz can or jar of Tahini (ground sesame seeds) 1 3/4 cups lemon juice
Blend in food processor or mixer until thoroughly blended, then refrigerate.	

Makes approximately 4 cups

Spinach in Sour Cream

What a yummy thing to do with spinach.

Carefully wash and stem the spinach leaves. Throw them into a pot of boiling water and boil no longer than 3 minutes.

Remove from pot and drain well. Melt butter in heavy pan. Add the flour, blend well.

Add spinach, onion, sour cream, salt and pepper. Heat thoroughly and serve immediately.

3 pounds young tender spinach

2 Tablespoons butter
1 Tablespoons flour

1 Tablespoons minced onion
1/4 cup thick sour cream
salt & pepper

Serves 6-8

Spicy Oven Fries

Less greasy than deep fried and tastes even better.

Preheat oven to 400°

6 medium russet potatoes

1/4 pound butter or margarine, melted
2 cloves pressed garlic
1/2 teaspoon. hot sauce
cayenne pepper to taste

Scrub potatoes and slice lengthwise into 8ths. Make small cuts across top of fries. In bowl, combine 6 tablespoons melted butter, garlic and hot sauce.

Toss potato spears in bowl with butter mixture and cayenne pepper until coated.

Place on baking sheet. Bake 30 minutes, or until done, basting once with any remaining butter mixture.

6-8 Servings

Coconut Milk Garlic Mashed Potatoes

The best potatoes for this are yellow Finn or Yukon gold.

Put potatoes in a pot with enough water to cover, boil until fork tender. Drain well.

Combine all ingredients in a food processor or mixing bowl until smooth.

Garnish with some parsley or a big dab of melting butter on top.

6 medium potatoes, (peeled & quartered)
1 cup milk
1/4 cup coconut milk
3 Tablespoons butter
3 cloves garlic (finely minced)
1 teaspoon salt
1/2 teaspoon pepper

8 Servings

"The coach became a pumpkin and the steeds turned back into mice, but Cinderella caught her prince despite it all. And they all went into therapy together."
　　Mama Colophon's Bedtime Stories

MAMA COLOPHON
(our founder)

Pumpkin Blueberry Corn Bread

A Fall treat for Thanksgiving or any other time

Preheat Oven to 350°
Spray 8" loaf pan with vegetable spray

Mix all ingredients except blueberries together in food processor or mixer until thoroughly blended. Fold blueberries gently into mixture

Bake 50 minutes or until center is done

3/4 cup whole wheat flour
1 teaspoon baking powder
1/2 teaspoon baking soda
1/2 teaspoon nutmeg
1/2 teaspoon cloves
1/2 teaspoon cinnamon
1/4 teaspoon salt
1/2 cup yellow corn meal
1/4 cup butter, softened
1/3 cup brown sugar
2 eggs
1/2 cup pumpkin puree
1/2 cup milk
1/2 cup blueberrries

Serve with Honey Rum Butter
Makes 1 loaf

Honey Rum Butter

Blend all ingredients and refrigerate.

Makes about 1/2 Cup

1 stick of butter
1 Tablespoon rum
1 Tablespoon honey
dash grated orange rind

(For Orange Butter, substitute Grand Marnier for the rum!)

Colophon Manager Dave Killian's grandfather grew the largest zucchini in the State of Washington in the 1970s. He has a special affinity for the vegetable.

Oregon Zucchini Cashew Bread

The poor zucchini, so popular, yet everyone wants to give you one, or two, or an entire box full.

Preheat oven to 350°. Spray two 8" loaf pans with vegetable spray Blend ingredients thoroughly in mixing bowl or food processor.

Sitr together dry ingredients in separate bowl and combine with first ingredients until blended.

Stir in cashews.

Bake 50 minutes or until center is done

3 eggs
1 cup canola oil
2 cups sugar or honey
2 cups grated zucchini
2 teaspoons vanilla

1 teaspoon baking soda
3 cups flour
1/4 teaspoons baking powder
1 teaspoon salt
2 teaspoons cinnamon
1 teaspoons nutmeg

1 cup cashews

Makes 2 loaves

Herbed Tomato Barbecue Sauce

The easy alternative to buying those bottled sauces that never quite taste the way you wish they would. Brush on vegetable skewers or use as a dipping sauce.

Stir all ingredients into large sauce pan. Bring to a boil, stirring occasionally to prevent burning.

Reduce heat and simmer 30 minutes.

Cool, place in covered containers and refrigerate throughly.

2-15 ounce cans tomato sauce w/bits
2 cups finely chopped sweet or yellow onion
1 cup dry red wine
3/4 cup dark corn syrup
5 cloves garlic, pressed or minced
2 teaspoons crushed dried basil
1 1/2 teaspoons thyme
1 teaspoon hot pepper sauce

Makes about 6 cups

Barbecued Vegetable Skewers

Prep this ahead of time and you'll have time to visit with guests instead of cooking.

Cut vegetables into large chunks, at least 2 inches square.

Arrange on metal skewers, alternating for color.

Place on hot barbecue grill and brush with sauce.

Cook 10 minutes and turn each skewer.

Cook 5-10 more minutes and serve hot.

2 large onions
1 green bell pepper
1 red bell pepper
1 medium zucchini, cut in half, seeds removed
10 mushrooms

Makes 4-6 skewers

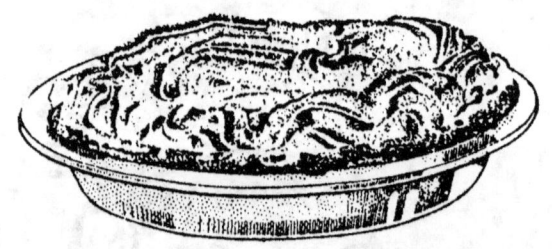

"Quiche me, you fool! thought Sleeping Beauty as she lay helplessly waiting for the handsome, but totally inept prince to get up the nerve to do it. I'll be stuck here forever, she moaned silently."
                Mama Colophon's Bedtime Stories

Quick Broccoli Cheddar Quiche

This is great brunch food! Serve with fresh fruit and little muffins and you've got it. Leftovers save well and are microwavable.

Pre-heat oven to 375°. Sprinkle flour in the bottom of a glass pie pan. Place pie crust in pan.

1 Tablespoon flour
One pre-made refrigerator pie crust at room temperature

Place in pie crust

1 cup chopped broccoli
1 cup grated cheddar cheese
1 cup grated mozzarella cheese

Beat together gently and pour over broccoli cheese mixture.

3 large eggs
1 1/2 cups 2% milk
1 Tablespoon cornstarch
1 teaspoon cayenne pepper
1 teaspoon hot dry mustard

Bake 40-50 minutes or until center is no longer liquid. Cool 15 minutes before serving.

Serves 6

Broccoli Cheddar Pot Pie

A rich and creamy pot pie with a parmesan biscuit topping. Great winter day food!

Preheat oven to 350.° Microwave ingredients on high until potatoes are soft; place into large bowl:

- 1/2 cup butter
- 1 lg onion, chopped
- 2 carrots, peeled & diced
- 3 celery stalks, sliced
- 2 large potatoes cut in small cubes
- 1/4 cup sherry
- 2 Tablespoons minced garlic

Microwave milk and cheese for 3 minutes, or until they can be blended together. Pour mixture over the vegetables

- 3 cups milk
- 1 cup grated cheddar or processed cheese spread

Add to vegetable mixture and mix thoroughly.

Scoop 1 1/2 cups of mixture into oven proof soup bowls. Top with parmesan biscuit rounds (recipe on next page). Brush with egg white.

- 50 oz canned cream of potato soup
- 1 cup cheddar cheese shredded
- 3 cups chopped broccoli (if using frozen, thaw first)
- 1/4 tsp white pepper
- 1/3 Tablespoon garlic powder

Bake for 20-25 minutes until bubbly and golden brown
Makes 6 large pot pies

Pot Pie Parmesan Biscuit Topping

Preheat oven 350°.
Mix ingredients on slow speed of mixer just until blended

2 cups flour
1 Tablespoon baking powder
1 teaspoon sugar
1/2 teaspoon salt
1/2 teaspoon pepper
1/2 teaspoon paprika
1/2 cup parmesan shredded
2 Tablespoons chopped green onions

Add butter pieces and mix until coarse. Blend in milk.

1/3 cup unsalted butter cut into 1/2 inch pieces
3/4 cup milk

Turn out onto a floured board and knead until the dough is no longer too sticky to work with.
Roll out dough to 1/4" thick.
Cut dough with paring knife, tracing around top of an upside down soup bowl.-Place biscuit rounds on the filled bowls.-Brush tops with egg whites.
Bake for 20-25 minutes until pot pies are bubbly and golden brown.

Makes 6 large pot pie toppings

Chili Relleno

Anaheim chili peppers have a delicate skin, therefore, when you peel the roasted peppers try not to tear up the flesh of the pepper, and don't worry about getting all the skin off.

Preheat broiler and roast chiles until blistered, about 5 minutes on each side.

Drain tofu and let sit for 5 to 10 minutes in a bowl. Drain again to remove excess water. Add garlic, salt, parsley, green onions and cheese. Blend in a mixer until creamy.

Mix baking soda with flour and whisk in soda water and 1/2 teaspoon salt until batter is thick and creamy.

Place peppers in a bowl or brown paper bag until cool enough to handle. Carefully peel off outer layer of charred skin and slice chili along the length of one side to remove seeds. Try to keep stems and pods intact if possible. Spoon some of the tofu filling and beans into each chili pod.

Heat 1/2 inch of oil in a large frying pan. Dip each chili in the batter until well coated. Fry in hot oil until golden brown (2-3 min. each side. Serve hot topped with the sauce of your choice.

10 fresh Anaheim chiles
1 pound. firm tofu
5 garlic cloves
2 teaspoon salt
1 cup parsley, chopped
1 bunch green onions, minced
1 cup grated jack cheese
1/2 cup flour
1/2 teaspoon baking soda
1 - 10 ounce bottle of soda water
1/2 teaspoon salt
1 1/2 cups refried black beans
1 cup corn oil

Serves 6

Sweet Onion Enchiladas

Prepare before a party and pull it out of the oven as everyone arrives. Great with salsa and sour cream on the side.

Preheat oven to 350°.

In bottom of 9" x 13" glass baking dish, spread 1/2 can hot enchilada sauce.

Warm other half can enchilada sauce in skillet. Using tongs, warm tortilla in sauce briefly on each side until soft but not falling apart and place gently in baking dish.

Fill with spoonfuls of cheese and onion, roll up, push toward the end of pan and repeat.

When baking dish is full, cover enchiladas with remaining can of mild enchilada sauce and jack cheese. Bake 20-30 minutes, or until bubbly.

1 can hot enchilada sauce
1 can mild enchilada sauce

2 cups grated jack cheese
1 cup grated cheddar cheese
1 cup chopped Walla Walla
   or other sweet onions

8 large corn tortillas

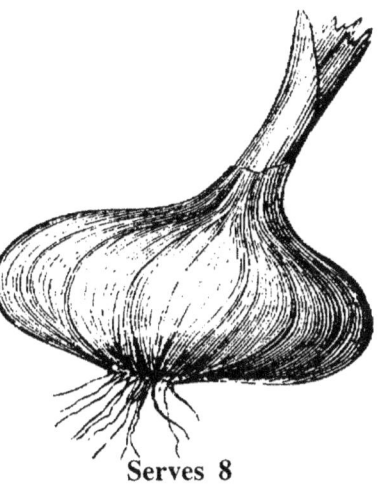

Serves 8

Jamaican Red Beans & Rice

A traditional, wonderful Jamaican dish.
Discovered on another one of Ray's exotic sailing trips.

In a sauce pan add coconut milk and water to the beans and rice, cover, bring to a boil and turn down to a simmer.

Cook until beans are tender. 1 to 1 1/2 hours

Add coconut, garlic, thyme chives and cloves, and simmer for another 30 minutes adding more water if it gets too thick.

2 cups canned coconut milk
4 cups water
3 cups white rice
1 cup red beans

1/4 cup dried coconut, grated
3 cloves garlic, minced
1 teaspoon thyme
3 Tablespoons chives, chopped
4 whole cloves

Serves 6

Spanakopita

*Contributed by Teresa Brainard,
waitstaff manager and fabulous cook!*

Preheat oven to 375°.
Saute onion and garlic in butter until lightly browned. Add spinach. Cook uncovered until tender and no liquid remains in pan.

Add nutmeg, salt and pepper, let cool.

Combine feta, egg, egg yolk and cream. Chop spinach mixture coarsely and stir into the egg mixture. Lay 1 sheet filo dough on flat surface, brush lightly with melted butter. Layer remaining 7 sheets over the first, brushing each layer lightly with the melted butter.

Spoon spinach mixture down long edge of filo dough. Fold up covering mixture, folding sides over about 1 inch. Roll up tightly, brush roll with butter. Place seam side down on baking sheet. Bake 20 to 25 minutes until golden brown, serve warm

1 Tablespoon butter
1 small onion, diced
2 cloves garlic, crushed

2 lbs fresh spinach

1/8 teaspoon nutmeg
salt & pepper to taste

1 cup feta cheese, crumbled
1 egg plus 1 egg yolk
3 Tablespoons cream

1/2 cup melted butter
8 sheets filo dough

Serves 6

Black Bean Taquitos con Guacamole

These are great hot, cold or any where in between

In a small frying pan heat oil until a drop of water sizzles when placed in it. Put a tortilla in, frying lightly on both sides. Fry just enough so that it is still pliable but not at all crisp. Remove from the pan to a paper towel and blot off any excess oil.

Gently combine all ingredients for the black bean filling. Put a small amount of the filling on one end of the tortilla. Roll it up and hold it together with one of the toothpicks. Place it in a baking dish and put in oven on low. Repeat process until all the Taquitos are in the oven.

Serve on a bed of lettuce. Top with chunky guacamole and crumbled cheese. Serve salsa on the side.

12 corn tortillas
1/2 cup corn oil

Black bean filling
1 cup cooked black beans
2 Tablespoons minced onion
1 teaspoon ground cumin
2 teaspoon chili powder
1 small tomato, chopped fine
12 wooden tooth picks

Garnish
1 cup shredded lettuce
1 cup guacamole
1 cup feta cheese
1 cup salsa

Serves 6

Chunky Guacamole

Gently mix all ingredients in bowl with fork.

If you are not serving the guacamole right away cover tightly with clear wrap, pushing the wrap lightly onto the mixture to keep it from turning dark, then refrigerate until used.

2 large avocados peeled and chopped
1/2 large white, sweet onion, chopped
1/2 teaspoon cumin
1 teaspoon chili powder
Dash garlic salt
1 Tablespoon lemon juice

Serves 6

Asian Noodle Salad

Fast and yummy.

Combine in large bowl

1 Tablespoon sugar
3 Tablespoons lime juice
3 Tablespoons water
3 Tablespoons soy sauce
2 Tablespoons creamy peanut butter
4 crushed garlic cloves

Boil noodles according to directions on box.

6 ounces uncooked spaghetti noodles

Toss hot noodles with peanut sauce. Add sprouts, green onions and peanuts.

1/2 cups bean sprouts
1/3 cup sliced green onions
1 cup dry roasted, unsalted peanuts

Serve warm in large bowls with chopsticks.

Serves 2

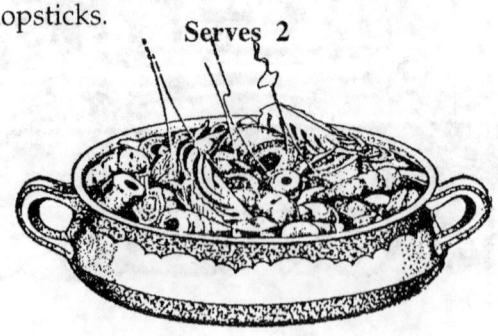

Mushroom Casserole

A quick and easy cold weather delight for mushroom lovers. Try it with different kinds of mushrooms, porto bellos are my favorite, but shitakes are also grand.

Preheat oven to 450.°
Cream seasonings thoroughly into butter. Spread a part of this butter mixture on the bottom of a casserole dish, arrange on mixture the mushroom caps, open side up. Dot each cap with some of the remaining butter mixture until all is used. Add the cream, salt and pepper. Bake for 10 minutes. Serve at once.

1/3 cup butter
1 teaspoon parsley, minced
1 teaspoon chives, minced
1 teaspoon onion juice
1 teaspoon salt
1/4 teaspoon cayenne pepper
1 teaspoon nutmeg
1/2 teaspoon tarragon
1 cup cream
salt & pepper to taste
18 large mushrooms
 (washed and stemmed)

Serves 6

"*In the spring a young man's fancy lightly turns to thoughts of love...*"
    Alfred Lord Tennyson, 1809-1892

"*...and thoughts of pie.*"
    Mama Colophon's Bedtime Stories

MAMA COLOPHON
(our founder)

"*Kiss till the cows come home*",
Beaumont & Fletcher, 1616
The Scornful Lady, act III

Finnish Apple Pie

Taimi's grandparents came from Finland and her grandma was a cook, so she tends to collect recipes from the far north. This one, fortunately, does not contain fish heads or any of the stuff Grandma used to use.

Pre-heat oven to 450°.
Blend cheese into the pie crust dough. Split dough in half and roll out for pie. Place one in pie pan and trim edge, leaving 1/2 inch all around.

Combine sugar and seasonings and toss with apples.

Layer apples into the pie crust and dot with butter. Sprinkle with lemon juice and peel.

Foll out remaining pastry and place on top of pie. Seal and flute edges. Make several slits on top.

Bake 10 minutes at 450°, then reduce heat to 375° and bake one hour longer until crust is golden.

pastry for a 9-inch double crust pie
1 1/2 cups shredded Finnish cheese-(or Swiss will do)

6 medium sized tart apples, peeled and sliced thin
1 peach, peeled and sliced
1 cup brown sugar
1 Tablespoon cinnamon
1 teaspoon allspice
1/4 teaspoon salt
2 Tablespoons soft butter
1 Tablespoon lemon juice
1/2 teaspoon grated lemon peel

Serves 6

Peach Oat Crisp

A fragrant dessert to serve hot out of the oven.

Preheat oven to 375°.
Put two tablespoons butter in bottom of 9"x 13" pan. Place in oven until butter melts. Pull from oven and spread melted butter evenly over bottom of pan.
Arrange peaches in an even layer.

In a bowl, combine brown sugar, flour, oats, cinnamon and nutmeg, blend in remaining butter with a fork. Mixture should be crumbly. Sprinkle evenly over peaches, pressing slightly with fork to cover top.
Bake 30-40 minutes or until fruit is tender.

May be topped with whipped cream, vanilla ice cream or served just as it is!

1/2 cup softened butter
3 pounds (6 cups) sliced peaches

1/2 cup brown sugar
1/2 cup flour
3/4 cup rolled oats
1/2 teaspoon cinnamon
1/2 teaspoon nutmeg

6-8 Servings

Pumpkin Pone

Pumpkin pone is a favorite confection of children of all ages in Guyana.

Preheat oven to 375°.
Blend pumpkin and coconut together in a medium bowl.
Add cornmeal and blend in margarine.
Add all other ingredients, and mix well. It should be a soft dripping consistency.

Pour into a greased 9"x12" baking pan. The mixture should be 1 to 1 1/2" thick.

Bake uncovered about 20 to 25 minutes or until crisp and brown.
Cut into 2" squares. May be served warm or cool.

1 pound pumpkin, grated
1/2 pound dried coconut, grated
1 cup cornmeal
2 oz. margarine
1/4 cup sugar
1 cup water
1/2 teaspoon cinnamon
1/4 teaspoon grated nutmeg
1/2 teaspoon vanilla extract
dash of salt

Dave's Breakfast Cookies

*Low-fat cookies created by Colophon Chef Dave Killian.
These make great tasting healthy snacks.*

Preheat oven to 325°. Mix together in mixing bowl	1 1/2 cups applesauce 1 1/8 cups brown sugar 1/2 cup apple juice 1/6 cup orange juice 1/6 cup lemon juice 2 Tablespoons vanilla
Mix in	1 mashed banana
Stir in	3/4 cup flour 1/2 cup wheat flour 1 Tablespoon baking soda 1/2 Tablespoon cinnamon 1/2 Tablespoon nutmeg 1/2 Tablespon ginger 3/4 teaspoon cloves
Stir in	4 cups oats 2 cups rice crispies 3/4 cup crushed corn flakes 3/4 cup dried fruit

These cookies are very moist. It is easiest to use an ice cream scoop and drop the dough on a parchment lined cookie sheet. Dip fingers into water and pat cookies into flat circles. They will not spread while baking.
Bake for 12-15 minutes.

Makes 24 Cookies

Bapple Cookies

Like "trail mix" in a cookie, many people eat just these instead of a full lunch!

Preheat oven to 350 degrees. Cream together in a large bowl	3/4 cup butter 3/4 cup white sugar 1/2 cup brown sugar 3 eggs, added one at a time
Add	3/4 teaspoons vanilla 1/2 cup apple juice 1/8 cup cooled espresso or very strong coffee
Mix together	2 1/2 cups flour 2 teaspoons baking soda 1/2 teaspoon salt 1/2 teaspoon allspice 1/2 teaspoon nutmeg 2 teaspoons cinnamon 3 3/4 cups oats
Stir in and mix well, scraping sides and bottom of bowl	1 medium chopped apple 3/4 cup raisins 3/4 cup chocolate chips 1/2 cup chopped walnuts

Drop rounded spoonfuls of dough onto parchment lined cookie sheet.
Dip fingers into cold water and press cookies into round, flat patties. (They will not spread while baking.)
Sprinkle each with 1/2 teaspoon chopped walnuts.
Bake 10-12 min or until light to med brown.
Do not overcook.

Makes about 2 dozen large cookies

Colophon Peanut Butter Pie

This pie is so delicious, "Bon Appetit" magazine requested our recipe and printed it in the August 1993 issue. This recipe makes 2 pies.

Mix together in a large bowl and set aside.	18 oz cream cheese 1 1/2 cups crunchy peanut butter 1 1/2 cups brown sugar
Whip on low speed for two minutes in chilled bowl Add sugar and whip on high speed until peaks form (do NOT overwhip or cream will turn buttery!)	1 teaspoon vanilla 2 cups heavy whipping cream 1/2 cup powdered sugar
Fold the whipped cream mixture into the peanut butter mixture.	

Spoon Mixture into two 8 inch Chocolate Cookie Crusts. Spread evenly and freeze pies for 3 hours.

Recipe continued on next page...

continued...

Melt in separate bowl

2 cups melting chocolate (or semi-sweet chocolate chips) with 1/2 cup half & half in the microwave for 30-45 seconds. Stir until smooth

Carefully spoon half the chocolate ganache on the top of each frozen pie. Spread evenly and quickly garnish with 1 Tablespoon chopped peanuts before the chocolate sets. Chill for 1 hour before cutting. Use a knife dipped in hot water for cutting.

This recipe makes two pies.
They may be frozen for storage.
To thaw, place in refrigerator for several hours.
They will cut more easily if partially frozen.

Chocolate Cookie Crust
For the Colophon Peanut Butter Pie

Combine well by hand or food processor

4 1/2 cups finely ground chocolate cookie crumbs
1/2 cup butter, melted

Divide in half and press into 2 pie tins. Bake 7-10 min at 350°.

Peanut Butter Chocolate Brownies

An invention by Taimi, these brownies are made in individual muffin cups for easy serving.

Preheat oven to 350°. Spray 2 one-dozen muffin tins with vegetable spray.

Blend ingredients in bowl or food processor.

Fold in flour and baking powder.

Add 1/2 package of chocolate chips to mixture. Spoon dough into muffin molds and bake 25 minutes.

Remove from oven and while still hot, spread remaining chocolate chips over each brownie. Let sit for five minutes and then spread melted chocolate with a knife.

2/3 cup softened butter
1 cup softened peanut butter
1 1/4 cups sugar
1 1/4 cups brown sugar
1 teaspoon vanilla
3 eggs
8 ounces sour cream

2 cups unsifted flour
2 1/2 tsp baking powder

1 16 ounce package chocolate chips

1 12 ounce package peanut butter chips

Garnish top of each brownie with peanut butter chips. Cool brownies overnight before removing from pan.

Makes 24 Brownies

Mom's Jamocha Rum Cake

Taimi's busy Mom likes things that are fast to make. This cake tastes like it took much more work than it did and it's one of the best you'll ever have.

Spray 9"X13" pan with vegetable spray.
Prepare cake mix as noted on the box. Mix in instant coffee, pour batter in pan and bake until done.
In saucepan, combine water, sugar, butter and rum. Heat until sugar disolves and butter is melted.
Make small cuts across top of cake with sharp knife. Spoon sauce over hot cake just out of oven.

Cool cake before topping. In chilled bowl, whip cream, sugar, instant coffee and cocoa together until it peaks. Frost cake, sprinkle with shaved chocolate and chill in refrigerator until served.

Cake
1 package moist devils food cake with pudding
1 Tablespoon instant coffee or espresso

Rum Sauce
1/2 cup water
1/2 cup sugar
2 Tablespoons butter
1/2 cup dark rum

Topping
2 cups whipping cream
3 Tablespoons powdered sugar
1 Tablespoon instant coffee or espresso
1 Tablespoon unsweetened cocoa
Grated or chopped milk chocolate

Makes one cake.
10-12 Pieces

Alphabetical Index

Best Vegetarian Recipes

MAMA COLOPHON

Almond Bean Soup	23
Asian Noodle Salad	66
Avocado Caesar Salad	35
Baked Almond Brie	9
Bapple Cookies	75
Barbecued Vegetable Skewers	53
Black Bean Taquitos con Guacamole	64
Broccoli Cheddar Pot Pie	58
Cheese Straws	10
Chili Cheese Dip	13
Chili Relleno	60
Chili Relleno Cheese Bars	6
Chilled Vegetable Pasta Salad	37
Chocolate Cookie Crust	77
Chunky Guacamole	65
Cinnamon Rice	43
Coconut Milk Garlic Mashed Potatoes	47
Colophon Croutons	17
Colophon Peanut Butter Pie	76
Corn Fritters	11
Dave's Breakfast Cookies	74
Finnish Apple Pie	71
Finnish Wilted Cucumber Salad	29
Galloping Guacamole	2
Gazpacho	18
Green Bean & Tomato Salad	32

Hawaiian Rice	42
Herbed Tomato Barbecue Sauce	52
Honey Rum Butter	49
Hummus	44
Jamaican Red Beans & Rice	62
Jumping Jalapenos	5
Mexican Corn & Bean Sopa	19
Moms' Jamocha Rum Cake	79
Mushroom Casserole	67
Orange & Radish Salad	31
Oregon Zucchini Cashew Bread	51
Peach Oat Crisp	72
Peanut Butter Chocolate Brownies	78
Pigeon Peas Accra	7
Pot Pie Parmesan Biscuit Topping	59
Potato Cheese Salad	36
Pumpkin Blueberry Corn Bread	49
Pumpkin Pone	73
Quick Broccoli Cheddar Quiche	57
Spanakopita	63
Spicy Quesadillas	3
Spicy Oven Fries	46
Spicy Peanut Sauce	40
Spicy Thai Rice Soup	21
Spinach in Sour Cream	45
Split Pea Soup w/croutons	17
Sweet Onion Enchiladas	61
Syrian Lentil Soup	25
Turkish Cucumber Salad	28
Vegetarian Potstickers	41

To order more books, phone
Village Books 1-800-392-BOOK

MAMA COLOPHON
(our founder)

www.ingramcontent.com/pod-product-compliance
Lightning Source LLC
Chambersburg PA
CBHW051941290426

44110CB00015B/2064